Common Sense
Learning and Living

John H. Hitchcock

Table of Contents

DEDICATION

This book is dedicated to all those fine people who fully understand

THE MIND MATTERS MOST

and real learning should last a lifetime.

Dedicated to teachers, administrators, parents and students who know this to be true but feel trapped or restricted by the nature of both the educational system and society at large.

Dedicated to those who know the system is flawed, and are ready to choose courage to create the initiative or actions necessary to rev

FOREWORD

The author of this book, John Hitchcock, has been a personal friend since rooming together in college our junior and senior years. On reflection, at that time I would not have expected to be writing this foreword. However, my having been involved in education, as elementary and secondary student, in my undergraduate and graduate studies, as a teacher of thirty-plus years both in this country and in Africa, and serving a university as a Field Supervisor of Student Teachers of social studies over 55 years of my life, I have a similar background to John's.

It is my good fortune to have been blessed with an innately indefatigable curiosity. I concur with Dorothy Parker's observation: "The cure for boredom is curiosity, There is no cure for curiosity." I know John would agree and woven throughout the book is the notion that curiosity is a fundamental element in attaining the end to which he writes.

John's analysis of his family relationships is spot on. I have come to know all of them and will attest that stimulating conversation and repartee was always the modality as we shared around a table or campfire.

The introductory quotes of eminent authors prepare the stage for each essay to follow. The author seamlessly blends the disciplines of sociology, science and religion into a composite package which, if adhered to, should lead to the proposed outcome: radical excellence.

Two main recurring themes set the tone:

The Mind Matters Most

and

You (can) Control Your Destiny.

If a parent, teacher, or administrator, anyone in a mentoring relationship, does not subscribe to those two propositions, whatever else emanates through or from that alliance will not approach radical excellence. Coupled with that desire to achieve, I subscribe to the author's postulation that a solid relationship with the Creator is concomitant to success. My personal coming to faith at age 19 enhanced that innate curiosity.

In this work, the author surveys the educational past, recounting unsuccessful efforts to 'fix' the system. As John states: The ultimate 'fix' involves parents, teachers and administrators who have the 'converted' heart and desire to see our educational system address the needs of future generations of children.

I think kids are great; and when one relates to them as viable human beings who need loving guidance in their formative years, there is great joy and satisfaction in teaching. Inculcating the elements of radical excellence is foundational to that end.

If the interested reader can absorb the essence of this book and implement the proposals in practice in whatever role they have, — student, parent, teacher or administrator, — that child and the educational venue will be the better for it.

Once grasped, striving for radical excellence will be rewarding and even fun!

David C. Schwedt,
Gowanda, NY
August, 2020

ACKNOWLEDGMENTS

I have always perceived Acknowledgments at the beginning of a book as a perfunctory exercise designed to make a few people feel good. Having written this book, then reflecting on the why and wherefore of doing it, I recognize the profound effect people have had on who I am and the way I think. It's with that in mind that I offer my genuine thanks and gratitude for the broad spectrum of people who have radically affected my life and being, and in their unique way, contributed to this book.

Without my wife, there's no book. She has listened to years of rants, raves and musings. Continuing to accept me, even in all my failures, she gave encouragement and advice that has been invaluable.

Our son and daughter and their spouses contributed an unlimited supply of opinions and coffee as we debated the subtle nuances of the learning world. Thanks so much to Greg & Charlene Hitchcock and Marla & Dario Pascarelli.

Influence starts early, and my mother and father taught me to think. Not only to think, but to be brave and simplistic enough to express those thoughts properly and publicly, thus developing the courage to risk success while not fearing failure.

My sisters and their husbands made life enjoyable as ideas and opinions flowed wildly in any discussion. Special thanks to Dave and Bonnie Newton and John and Sharon Hayes. Special thanks to Dave for all those golfing and barn-building times where educational discourse still could prevail.

The In-law group has been equally stimulating. It's rewarding to have lived around people with strong and vigorously expressed opinions. Life is much more intriguing because of that. Thanks to Ron & Kathie Pagano-Fuller and Don and Liz Hamilton.

The "Carlson Clan" of aunts, uncles and cousins who brought imagination and humor to life simply by living deserves extreme thanks.

Two special cousins taught me that laughter doesn't have to be trivial and thinking isn't a chore. Thank you, Dan Saulsgiver and Earl (always will be "Sam") Hitchcock.

The other members of our now widely dispersed teaching and golfing foursome leave me with hilarious memories of golf and amazingly deep remembrances of educational philosophy. Thank you, Clint Radford, Willie Guida and Steve Hoff. See you on the back nine.

Many of the people I've worked with have stretched my brain and fostered wonderfully new ideas. Donn Headley and Beth Smith remarkably so, and I continue to miss our morning chats before the world really got started.

The west-coast contingent of colleagues who have contributed include Bruce Prins, John Shoup, Kevin Aley, and Tricia Higgins. The most recent Westerners, Dr. Stephen Pietrolungo and the "Room 16" contingent of Rosanna Giordani-Clegg, Cindy Madden, Stacey Zielinski and Ali Taverner.

The other-coast group includes Clay Auwarter, Dale LaQuay, Martha Bennett, and Catherine Bell. Their impact on my thinking surfaces frequently throughout this book.

Someone who's not even close to the box in thinking is Dave Schwedt, my roommate in college. His ideas and those of his wife, Kathy, gave freedom and fruition to ideas. Thanks for doing that.

There is another eclectic group of people whose own form of radical excellence quietly influenced those whom they encountered. Rev. Lloyd Newton, James Jordan, John Riley, Joe Herney, Alice Ives, Hugh Paine, Frieda Gillette, Rev. Angell, Archie "Bobcat" Ranney, Gordon Stockin and Richard Troutman brought things to my life that ultimately helped forge philosophy and pragmatism into action.

I have been blessed to be alive in contact with such an enthusiastic and inspirational group of people.

Thank you all.

Chap. 1 - Why I write this book

There are risks and costs to action.
But they are far less than the
Long range risks of comfortable inaction.

John F. Kennedy

When I was seventeen years old I sold chickens and cut brush to buy my first car, a 1957 four-door Ford sedan. The odometer had broken at 101,000 miles, the back doors would often stick closed and the rocker panels were more rust than metal.

Coming home from fishing one day I saw the vivid bright green of seemingly new rocker panels. My father was standing nearby and as I walked over to give the new panels an admiring kick, he said, "Careful. Don't do that. It's duct tape."

The temporary fix of duct tape on rust didn't solve the underlying problem of deteriorated rocker panels. The car was improved cosmetically, but the defect still existed. Symptoms were hidden for a while... the problem remained.

The world of school.

Educational fixes often seem to offer the same method of solving inherent problems. More money, more technology, more training, more online classes, more acronyms; the list of shiny new objects purporting to fix foundational problems keeps growing. Each new thing a "duct tape" patch on a system with fundamental flaws.

These expensive, publisher-driven fixes focus on content with some well-intentioned attempts to address higher order aspects of learning. STEM, STEAM, SEC and Common Core attempt to provide a system of teaching and learning to ensure success on standardized exams. As politicians and publishers compete, the educational system begins to resemble a Duct Tape-covered spectrum of acronyms.

Life in the "Real World."

Actually, school and the real world are not different, yet we seem to treat life that way. What kids learn, or "not learn," in school affects who they are as people. Similarly, family life, "hanging out" with friends, job interactions, all merge into the dynamic we call life.

Problems and possibilities abound, and we seem to always be reacting to both rather than being assertive in choosing the path of living that is best for us.

We don't need more duct-tape.

We need a radical revolutionary change in the foundational system of learning and living. This revolution doesn't need to be adversarial. It doesn't have to be a top-down implementation. In fact, if a revolution in learning and living is to be successful, it MUST be initiated and continued at the grassroots level of being alive.

Significant change takes time. It takes commitment. And courage. Most of all, a genuine revolution needs to be fueled by a clear vision of what can be! To come to fruition, strategic actions must be implemented to bring victory to the stated goals.

There needs to be more cowboy in living!

Cowboys worked for the rancher, they did their job; tending the cattle, branding, rounding up, mending fence… yet each cowboy was his own man, an individual whose personal story invoked intrigue and admiration.

Our lives need to have a similar sense of adventure that is expectantly real to us. We need to do our parenting, living and careers properly, but must be courageous enough to adopt a radical form of excellence that creates memorable experiences as we interact with being alive.

Unfortunately, we are more often like cookie cutters than cowboys. Cut from the same tin mold, we line up as an array of entertainment consumers, wealth gatherers or "go with the flow" passengers in a constantly changing cultural universe.

Victimization or "Radical Excellence."

If you accept the fact that ***the mind matters most*** in everything we do, you will not consider yourself a victim or robotic follower of cultural mores. You will develop an intense desire to live with a radical excellence, defying the norm of living only for pleasure and self-indulgence.

By radical excellence I mean living your life in such a manner that your actions and attitude stand out positively from the normal culture in which we live. Character traits such as integrity, compassion, ambition, timeliness, respect and cheerfulness are consistently observed in your life and will set you apart from the norm of contemporary culture. Doing what you do with a consistent search for excellence will make your life a unique and positive example.

When we think deeply and logically about how we are doing life, our outlook on living changes. We see others differently, we analyze our choices with logic and purpose. As we begin to think deeply about our approach to life, somehow we may see an increase in our initiative and courage to make attempts to facilitate necessary changes.

As we muse on the realities of life, possibilities of positive change emerge. We begin to stop blaming the transitory "they" and choose the courage to speak up, maybe even take action, on things needing action.

Unfortunately our present culture tends to promote silence about crucial issues (who wants to be called "hater?") and the continued immersion in easy entertainment. The time has come for thinking and motivated people to realize individual action can have corporate results.

Robert Frost's poem reflecting his love relationship with his wife is interestingly relevant to the world of living and learning.

WEST-RUNNING BROOK

Robert Frost

Fred, where is north?"
"North? North is there, my love.
The brook runs west."
"West-running Brook then call it."
(West-running Brook men call it to this day.)
"What does it think it's doing running west
when all the other country brooks flow east
to reach the ocean? It must be the brook
can trust itself to go by contraries
the way I can with you—and you with me—
Because we're—we're—I don't know what we are.
What are we?"
"Young or new?"
"We must be something.

Going against the normal flow is risky. Colleagues may be derisive or think you marginally sane. Bosses may be offended… or worse. Your children may rebel at first, but soon adulthood kicks in and your radical excellence becomes apparent, accepted, even admired.

As you make mind-determined decisions, you may lose "friends." Those friends you lose because you made higher order decisions will almost always be replaced. New friends, new ideas and new purpose will become a natural part of your being alive.

Priming the Pump.

On my backpacking adventures in the Adirondack Mountains of New York state, there was one place where the only safe water came from an old-fashioned pump that needed priming. The sweaty, thirsty hiker had to take the jar of fresh water left by the previous person and pour it into the pump, creating the seal allowing the pump to bring fresh water to the surface.

Pouring the only water down the pump took a step of trust and confidence in bringing needed water to the hiker.

The purpose of this book is to prime our revolutionary learning, teaching and living pump. Let's take a leap of confidence and begin quietly creating a universal cultural revolution bringing a lifetime of passionate learning and purpose to our own lives and others.

On the day I turned fifty I wrote a simple, statement poem:

<u>The Hat</u>

When I get old
I don't want to be anything.
I just want to have a hat.
Not a plastic hat,
but one whose sweat-stained band
fits snugly in my furrowed brow.

I share that poem because it's important you know I am just a common guy. Just a normal, working, thinking and observing person.

A classroom career teaching physics and chemistry to teenagers could have made me jaded… maybe even frightened or pessimistic. But that is not the case.

One of my favorite authors, Harry Blamires, stated, "Idealists are the most tortured of all people."

I admit to being an idealist. Fortunately also an optimist! Nor is it counter-intuitive to be those and also a pragmatic realist.

From that perspective, I have been honored to work with many students and colleagues who represent the best of people. They have sparked my enthusiasm and created a strong base for my optimism.

Unfortunately I have also encountered a growing number of parents, students and colleagues who possess several cultural characteristics and ideas having the potential to destroy the foundational nature of learning and living, even without inventing a new acronym. Most importantly, as we destroy the places where education occurs, we are ultimately destroying our country.

And let's be clear; education occurs at school, but also at home and work and just hanging out with friends.

We are traveling a dangerous path, but one that doesn't shout out its danger. In fact, it is a rather pleasurable path. One quite enjoyable and filled with open acceptance and extreme pleasure.

And that's why I am writing this book.

Life changes as we change.

In November 22, 1963, I was a rookie teacher; enthusiastic, passionate, motivated, inspired, questioning almost nothing. John Kennedy's assassination wasn't the defining moment in my global thinking about the decline of our country and educational system, but it was the moment that initiated my thinking beyond the immediate surroundings I lived happily within.

I began thinking beyond the daily lesson plan and started developing a deep-rooted mechanism of living-out my chosen worldview.

It took about twenty years for me to clearly understand the ultimate meaning and basis of my own beliefs. I finally could express what I considered the foundational principles radically affecting our daily lives, especially within the context of educating the young people of our country.

Simply stated, who we are and who we are becoming, entails two practical ideas.

First, ***the mind matters most!*** Everything we do or how we react is determined by our minds.

Second, ***chosen decisions produce who wc are today,*** and decisions today determine our tomorrows.

I am more than a little hesitant to write this book.

We live in a politically correct, all-inclusive and morally relative society. Disagreement on almost any issue of importance gets one labeled a **hater** or simply dismissed as intellectually deficit. Many of the issues I shall address are politically incorrect and question the moral and ethical nature of much of our present culture.

I grew up in a family of independent thinkers, each of us rather animated in our own way. We could debate any issue openly and with strong opinions. Powerful debates, but NEVER an accusation of being a hater or any hint of lessening respect.

Some of the ideas expressed in this book fly in the changing face of culture. I do not expect all my friends and family to agree with me. I hold real hope that those who believe differently will not allow disagreement on significant issues lead them to think my love for them is diminished in the least.

Holding those fears is real, but I feel a greater compulsion to express my thoughts openly and honestly.

Foundations of Failure.

The general population is replete with criticism of the education system in our country. Recurring systemic complaints abound.

- "Graduation rates are way too low."
- "Young people have lost the ability to think critically or analytically."
- "Knowledge of our country or culture is seriously lacking."
- "Disrespect for those who disagree with us is rampant."
- "School curriculum is constantly being *dumbed down*."

It's important to understand those criticisms are NOT causes; they are simply symptoms of broader aspects of the changing culture in which we live.

It is my opinion our cultural difficulties, including the nature of education, parenting and cultural interactions, arise because of the significant influence of seven radical concepts in our corporate living.

- Evolution v. Intelligent Design
- Abortion v. Right to Life
- Gender Confusion v. Traditional Family
- Artificial Intelligence v. Personal Creativity
- Substance and Device Addiction v. Confident Living
- Political Correctness v. Open Dialogue
- Relativistic Thinking v. Absolute Truth

The purpose of this book is not intended to analytically and thoroughly address those concepts. Rather I hope to open the possibility of honest debate and dialogue. My idealism envisions a culture of open discussion focused on creating an educational culture producing genuinely successful students.

I must write.

What this book is NOT.

If you are expecting a data-driven, intensely researched document, this book is not for you.

If you are expecting a world-famous author, this book is not for you.

On the other hand, if you can accept a semi-radical, even controversial look at commonly accepted events in our lives and how they can be steps towards educational disaster… you will understand this book.

If you can accept something written by just a common guy, someone just like you… you will appreciate this book.

If you can accept a risky analysis of commonly accepted or enjoyable parts of our society… you may be enthused by this book.

By the way, there will be very little "moral of the story" in this book.

I will write basically the way I teach. My observations and examples will stand on their own. This is an experience-focused book. "Here's what I observe or think. The rest is up to you."

When former students talk about inspirational activities gleaned from "school" it's not about groups of teachers. It is almost always directed toward individual teachers. That is an important concept.

Thirty-six Years Later...

I read George Orwell's novel "1984" in 1959 as a senior in high school. Even then it created a sense of anticipation making the future ambiguous, even ominous.

1984 came without incident, a relief to many. But here we are in 2020 experiencing many of Orwell's imaginings; devices that listen, electronic recognition and a flat-screen society quietly dumbing us down.

As pandemic-induced online learning is diminishing personal interaction, are we as teachers becoming "Big Brother?" Or at least his precursor?

We **must** create a cultural revolution in education to prevent misguided individuals and artificial intelligence from hijacking the personal and human nature of educating our youth.

One more thing.

I am **not** writing this book to try and convert you to my way of thinking about the critical issues.

My challenge to you is simple; choose courage to listen to ideas which might be counter to yours. Listen with respect, respond in your own mind without rancor or meaningless rhetoric.

Use your mind, build your arguments, and let's have a dialogue.

The same challenge exists for those of you who do agree with me. Leave the normal intellectual dismissal behind of those you think are abandoning "traditional values." Listen without fear to ideas you find abhorrent. Turn your own rhetoric into reason. Most importantly, continue to speak the truth. Never give in to the rancor and ill-founded rhetoric of those who despise dialogue.

Only as we come together with constructive dialogue will our educational system improve and thus improve the stability and focus of our nation.

Read on.

Part 1 - America, we have a problem.

In response to hearing a loud bang and several warning lights appearing on the command console, Jim Lovell's character in the 1995 movie, *Apollo 13*, says, "Houston, we have a problem."

After analyzing the evidence, engineers on the ground concocted a fix, making the problem manageable, providing the astronauts a safe return to earth.

For decades the loud crash of ill-prepared students has sent the message **we have a problem** in American education. Multiple attempts have tried to fix the situation, yet every election cycle the noise of the problem is addressed one more time.

It is my belief the problem continues because we are not focused on the root causes of the educational disaster.

Part 1 expands on two underlying causes of the foundational problems we face in genuinely educating the youth of our country.

.

1. Intrinsic but subtle activities and attitudes
2. Issues caused by a Cultural Crisis

An old, weather-beaten house cannot be rejuvenated by simply applying a new coat of paint. An appropriate primer needs to be used, thus enabling the new paint to cling to the old wood.

Similarly, until we understand the underlying principles and problems confronting teaching and learning in this century, our efforts will flake off and need a new acronym based program, giving at most, a temporary "feel good" approach to solving the problem.

As you read, remember this… I am calling for a CULTURAL REVOLUTION in education. We need to choose the courage to take risks, seek wisdom and embrace radical change. This revolution can be enhanced and hastened by groups working together, but it absolutely starts with individuals acting bravely within their immediate sphere of influence.

John Hitchcock

Chap. 2 - Schools are Attacking Symptoms

We stigmatize mistakes. And we're now running national educational systems where mistakes are the worst thing you can make -- and the result is that we are educating people out of their creative capacities.

Sir Ken Robinson

In my experience as a teacher, early in the school year there is always the assessment and goal setting meeting. We are given statistical information that needs to be addressed during the next nine months.

- Our graduation rates are too low.
- Too many students were expelled or suspended.
- Math scores are still declining.
- The gap between minorities and white students grows.
- …and the problems go on.

Then the lamenting and whining of teachers begins.

- Whatever happened to good parenting?
- It's those d*@&*#d smartphones fault.
- How can we teach if the District won't give enough money?
- We absolutely need smaller classes.
- If I didn't need a second job, I could teach better.
- How can you teach when kids don't give respect.

Eventually, the District or State decides to adopt the newest "shiny object" program to solve all these problems. Publishers of revamped or politically motivated programs encourage adoption of their "new" ideas and techniques, promising great change... and massive profits.

- "Johnny can't read" may have started it.
- Then came "No Child Left Behind."
- "Every Student Succeeds" soon followed.
- We need "Professional Learning Communities."
- Let's try doing "Social-Emotional-Learning."
- And of course, the "Common Core" national program.

To achieve credibility, all the new programs must have the requisite acronym to make it sound important and memorable. Sometimes I suspect there is a federal or state division whose purpose is to create programs to go with the newly formed acronyms.

There is a major problem:

It isn't obvious, but almost all the recognizable problems inherent in the education process are the results of more fundamental failings of education itself and also inherent problems in the broader culture of living. It isn't just the world of education feeling the brunt of these failings, but these difficulties have a profound effect on the broader scheme of culture.

There are some illnesses where a physician will treat the symptom only. This gives some relief, but doesn't necessarily solve the real problem. It is my opinion we need to look more deeply into the root causes of problems in our school system and the negative components of everyday living. We need to start treating causes, not just hiding symptoms.

The Subtle Causes of a Quiet Chaos

John Wooden, the highly successful coach of UCLA basketball, said, *"Failure isn't fatal, but failure to change might be."* His words were within the context of basketball, but resonate powerfully for both an individual life and the existence of a broader culture.

In the world of chaos mathematics there exists the phenomenon of the strange attractor, a point of infinitesimal magnitude towards which plotted functions tend to converge. Interestingly, in some of these functions, a point of radical divergence occurs, and the plotted function goes screaming off into a new abstract universe where the nature of the graph changes radically.

The historical educational pendulum has always behaved itself, oscillating around its own fairly well defined attractors. Fundamental academic ability, universally accepted social values, concepts of thinking, all eventually attracted the swinging pendulum back to an acceptable modicum of educational performance.

I fear the current educational pendulum isn't coming back! I think we've reached the point of subtle, quiet chaos where the system is defining its own intrinsic principles and rules of education. As educators, we cling to a pendulum, but one whose path is no longer predictable and defined.

At times I picture educators in our own carnival of learning, standing at one of those game booths where obnoxious stuffed animals pop from various holes. We smack them back down with a wildly swung mallet, only to have another beast emerge from the next hole. In education we exist as symptom-smashers, blasting *can't read* animals down with our acronym labeled hammers only to have the *"can't do math"* animal emerge.

The simple fact is, we exist in an environment with high-potential kids, but with socially molded hearts. They come to our schools with unlimited potential... but polluted promises.

Have you ever noticed how disconcerting it is when someone else has the TV remote? Visual and mental chaos is created as they switch channels just as your mind is focusing in on your own interest.

That's how I've felt dealing with the students of our remote-control-generation. Just a momentary glimpse, then CLICK!... and a new event, a new deficiency surfaces.

"I hate that teacher"	CLICK!
"This course is hard"	CLICK!
"My job sucks"	CLICK!
"We aren't in love now"	CLICK!
"This is boring"	CLICK!

My fear is simple. Our students come to us with no solid conviction of the greater purposes of life. Even more ominous, the remote is in their hands. Compounding that fear, Dad and Mom keep supplying fresh batteries for the remote. In their quest to provide a good and safe life for their children, parents have acquiesced to being constant enablers.

"That assignment too hard? Okay, I'll call the teacher," they say.

"You missed the deadline to sign up for the field trip? That's okay. I will give them a call and I'm sure they'll still let you go." and once more the child is not given the opportunity to learn from the results of natural consequences.

Life is lived with the remote in hand. If an event or encounter isn't one I like, a simple push of the excuse button and on to the next more enjoyable event.

Booze, gangs, pre-marital sex and drugs are certainly difficulties and evils that need to be avoided by teens today. In my opinion, however, there are more insidious evils that need addressing. More insidious since they're quiet, appearing almost safe, yet corporately those evils join to produce a growing generation of students almost devoid of the most critical skills needed to live a productive and successful life.

The Flat Screen Generation

Students today are being raised by flat screens. TV, videos, computers, movies, video games, and cell phones create a concentrated culture of flat screens carrying messages requiring little thought or meditation. Almost everything kids watch today is at the shallowest, most emotional, level of interaction. Car chases, dragons to slay, and videos with startling images enter the eyes, titillate the emotions, and quickly transition to the next intense image. Nowhere does the watcher have the time to relax, muse, ponder or repeat.

Should we wonder then, why students struggle with critical thinking issues, panic when in-depth analysis is required, or shut down when readings contain polysyllabic words?

Flat screens rule. Not only do they rule, they consume. There was a day when little children woke up in the morning and did something. They played, they read, maybe even went and bugged mom and dad. Now, even very young children slip quietly from their bed, find the remote and sit transfixed on the floor as the every-morning cartoons (or worse) enter their eyes and infiltrate their minds.

As kids consume a continuing diet of visual stimulation followed by emotional reaction, they can kiss thinking goodbye.

Ray Bradbury predicted it. In *Fahrenheit 451.* The elimination of books had essentially demolished thinking. The burning of books had removed the concept of vision from the minds of people. Hope arose when Bradbury writes, "...Then he met a professor who told him of a future in which people could think...and Guy Montag suddenly realized what he had to do!"

We don't need to burn books to keep kids from reading. We don't even need to hide them. Just give the kid a TV-remote, iPod or video game player and the books go unread.

Francis Schaeffer warned us in *The Church at the End of the Twentieth Century* that "... men will end up owning only two values...personal peace and personal affluence." By personal peace he meant that men would hold to the concept of "let me do my own thing. Don't bug me." In Schaeffer's mind, personal affluence meant that men would have the economic ability to make entertainment and easy enjoyment very affordable.

The movie *Star Wars* launched an exciting new generation of graphics, and in so doing, may have generated a whole new way of absorbing information. One amazing special effect after another kept us on the edge of our seats, not thinking, but reacting. Movies started advertising the special effects, often more than plots or story lines.

So what's the big deal? What's intrinsically wrong with great action? What can be harmful about amazing car chases or explosions?

For starters, God wrote to us. He really did. And books require reading. I know that's a simple thought, but it's true. It isn't just God-words, either. Ideas are communicated by rather lengthy written discourse. For example, the philosophies and ideas of an American

Revolution did not occur by a series of ten-second sound bites on the evening news, but were transmitted by extensive publication and distribution of revolutionary pamphlets.

People read books and pamphlets... and the world was changed. Now, movie stars, musicians and famous athletes promote often harmful ideas... and our kids listen and believe.

Having Learned the "Not"

Once upon a time, in a land that's gone forever, kids actually knew about responsibility and acted that way. Not all, of course, but most seemed to understand and accept the absolute worth of appropriate behaviors in the area of accountability, work ethic, and accepting consequences of actions.

Then society progressed. Mom started working outside the home, and the number of kids who acted responsibly shifted slightly. Many kids still acted properly, but an ever-increasing number began to act counter to what they knew to be right. Their behavior was frustrating, but because they knew the right way, that behavior was fairly easily fixed.

Then came the nineties. Entertaining technology grew exponentially, single parent families became more common, radical-isms and political correctness were socially imposed, and comprehensive acceptance of a broadly defined diversity changed the way we looked at the idea of right and wrong. Now in the twenty-first century we have students living lives counter to the positive characteristics that have been philosophically and historically based.

Students now come to school having learned how to be NOT responsible, NOT polite, etc. Profoundly more important than what's *not* taught is the inevitable learned lesson.

Let me illustrate with a basketball lesson.

One day on lunch duty I watched three of my basketball players doing some mild practicing in a one-on-one game on our outdoor court. When they finished, I called them over.

"Good job, gentlemen. Nice shooting practice." I said.

"Hey, thanks." they replied, pleased that I had noticed.

"By the way, you were very effective at practicing two things other than just shooting." I continued.

"Really. What's that?" they asked, surprisingly intrigued.

"Well, for one thing, you did a great job at practicing *not* blocking out your opponent when he shot. Furthermore, you also really perfected the technique of *not* following your shot." I said.

The point is simple. Our students come to us knowing how to use their "remotes" to make life choices easier, and they also come having learned their lessons well. Too bad it's the WRONG lesson. They have learned that NOT doing homework is okay, that NOT studying for a test the first time only leads to "credit recovery" systems, and almost any other NOT characteristic you can think of.

CRITICAL THINKING can be learned. That is a fact, and one that many, if not most, teachers ascribe to. Considerable energy and effort is expended in classrooms trying to impart that skill into students. Trouble is, all those negative attributes contribute to a lessening ability of students being able to learn how to think critically. Unfortunately, there are also some subtle characteristics that can exist in teachers, administrators and the entire system that compound the difficulty of teaching critical thinking even further.

Approval by Acquiescence

Sometimes my neurological synapses operate slower than I would hope, so it's taken me a while to verbalize some of my thoughts about trash.

It all started with another of my many days on the ever-present lunch duty. I was on one side of the outdoor lunch area and observing the other teacher on duty as he was telling a table of ninth grade boys that their table trash was unacceptable. Having given the appropriate reprimand, the teacher turned and walked towards the gate. From my vantage point, I watched one of the boys deliberately and flauntingly flick a piece of garbage from the table to the concrete floor.

Old bones moved faster than I'd prefer, and momentarily the

gentlemen and I were discussing the matter in a rather adversarial mode. The boys soon realized that they were, in fact, going to police the entire area, and as they worked, my thoughts slowly started crystallizing.

My next class after lunch was normally rather talkative before class began, and this day was no exception. Three or four mini-conversations were occurring, and just as I began telling them to focus in on the thought for the day my mind went into Far Side cartoon mode. Suddenly it seemed to me that their words in this time of chatting became like pieces of trash emanating from their mouths and falling randomly to the floor.

For some reason the following thought flashed through my mind.

By acquiescing to that which is unacceptable, we give tacit approval to that action. We give approval not only to those doing the unacceptable action, but an implied approval to those who only sit and watch. Approval is granted to their "sitting and watching" as much as it is to the unacceptable act.

By ignoring a problem we are actually proactive in teaching a message, and the message is that corporate responsibility is not in the domain of individual activity. Thus, that which is individually unacceptable suddenly becomes acceptable in the greater, corporate sense. In the lunch area event, I'm confident that each individual would agree that it's wrong to throw their trash on the ground, yet by acquiescing to letting it happen, we have approved and taught that as an acceptable action.

Even more importantly, had I done nothing and other students watched me do nothing, I would have taught the lesson it's okay to stand by and not address things that are wrong.

Law of Unintended Consequences

One of the standard safety practices when hiking or backpacking with a group is that the weakest hiker, the one who will lag behind, is always accompanied by a stronger, more experienced hiker. The weaker hiker is never left to fend alone at the back of the group. In accompanying the weaker hiker, however, the more experienced person must operate at a diminished level of skill in order to accompany the novice. In this case, the stronger hiker willingly stays at the back as a protective measure.

In most things we do there is an obvious distribution of skill and ability level, and the obvious observation in the backpacking world is that at some prior time the stronger hiker had been given the opportunity to risk... to venture ahead... unfettered by acquiescing to the norm. Someone, somehow had enthused the stronger to become just that, to learn the techniques and acquire the stamina to lead the pack. And now the stronger can actually help the weaker become better.

In an ideal world, no one would ever be left behind. Life isn't ideal, however, and a normal distribution of skills and abilities naturally occurs. Someone is always the fastest, another the slowest. Some do calculus, others are hard-pressed to multiply double digit numbers.

The national intent to leave no child behind was well-intended, but statistically impossible to attain. We attempt that Herculean task by establishing curricular "*STANDARDS*" that can hopefully be achieved by everyone. Then we attempt to measure the successful attaining of those standards by using the oft worshiped and frequently cursed Standardized Test. (notice... said with appropriate awe)

For the sake of economy and speed, those standardized tests were almost totally multiple-choice questions. The Number 2 pencil and the Bubble Sheet became the implements of war in the fight to achieve an acceptable level of academic performance. Not only are individuals measured by these exams, but also the performance levels of individual schools and teachers is directly tied to how well the students perform on these semi-sacred tests.

The commendable emphasis on establishing academic standards and measuring performance by standardized tests may have resulted in an unfortunate and insidious unintended consequence. Just as our students think at the flat-screen level, they analyze in the multiple-choice mode.

Kids are not stupid. They might not pass math or be able to write an interesting paragraph, but they sure do know how to take multiple-choice exams. The trouble is, their idea of "taking" a multiple-choice test isn't what the testers envisioned. Students have learned how to do a cursory reading of the question, quickly eliminate two answers because they "look wrong," and then make a supposedly reasonable guess at the right answer.

For the past several years I have conducted an interesting exercise which substantiates that hypothesis. I select several questions that would normally be multiple choice questions on standardized tests. These selected questions all have answers that are definitive or can be calculated precisely using the proper formulas. I then blacken in all the choices, but leave them on the test so it's obvious that they are of the multiple choice variety. Sadly, the majority of the students react with, "We can't do these! The answers are all blocked out!" And unfortunately, they're right! Most of them are literally unable to perform at a passing rate on this type of doctored exam, even though the basic knowledge to do the questions is within their framework of learned material.

The importance of doing well on these exams can't be ignored. Graduation, acceptance into college, school evaluation and teacher performance are all evaluated based on often ill-prepared students taking curricular exams using faulty methods.

Life is decidedly not ideal.

Teachers are apt to fall into the mode of testing almost exclusively in a multiple-choice fashion. The extensive practice on weekly tests is thought to produce a comfort level for the students when they take the standardized exams. Another compelling factor encouraging multiple-choice testing is the efficiency of grading when class sizes approach the imponderable and unworkable in many schools.

Having lived with and experienced this syndrome as it developed through teaching in five different decades, I am led to the conclusion that an ironic result of creating artificial standards and testing incessantly with multiple-choice questions has inadvertently resulted in an overall lessening of critical thinking and analytical abilities. Ironically, emphasizing a multiple-choice style of testing ultimately results in a lessening of the very thinking and learning processes the system was intended to improve.

Internet Information Ignorance

Several years ago some studies indicated that the amount of knowledge was doubling about every ten years. I suspect it might take less time in our present age of research and discovery. In fact, Peter Large of Information Anxiety says, "More information has been produced in the last 30 years than in the previous 5,000. About 1,000 books are published internationally every day, and the total of all printed knowledge doubles every eight years."

I do know that the amount of knowledge immediately available is vastly greater than the nostalgic era when many homes had at least one shelf of the living room bookcase filled with a neat arrangement of the encyclopedia just purchased from the door-to-door salesman.

To illustrate the preponderance of information, a few years ago, I gave a physics assignment in which the students were to choose a common technological device, investigate the primary physics principles on which the device depended, then write an analysis of how that device had influenced societal behavior, either positively or negatively.

One student selected the flush toilet as her technological focus. After finishing her Internet research, she cited six separate sites devoted entirely to the operation of the flush toilet.

I'm going to suggest that you won't find six pages of information about toilets in any of the shelved encyclopedias.

This girl was a unique student, however. She actually read and analyzed the downloaded pages.

The norm of student Internet research is a bit different, as illustrated in the extreme by another student who wrote a social studies paper on the city of London, England.

His paper consisted of a Title Page and then twenty-six pages of downloaded and printed Internet information stapled together. When the teacher confronted him about this rather simplistic method of writing a research paper, the student defended his work by saying, "But I did the research. Look at that. I've got twenty-six pages of stuff. What more do you want?"

Obviously that's the extreme, but it's more representative of the kind of research and analysis many students perform. They Google a topic, take a perfunctory glance at the first few hits, then copy and paste some marginally relevant paragraphs. Of course the paper isn't complete until they paste in a few totally plagiarized and un-cited pictures or diagrams from the website.

Partly as a result of Approval by Acquiescence, Students have *learned the not* of a click-and-copy mode of research at the same shallow level of learning they use to take multiple choice examinations.

Avoiding Institutional Inertia

At some point in time, kids started going to a place called school. These places of learning strongly reflected the societal wishes of the historically traditional family. Times were simpler, and learning consisted of the mastery of a closely defined body of knowledge generally considered intrinsic in educated people.

Knowledge entwined with education often promotes activism in thinking. Certain aspects of this educated society then began to create a technologically based culture, the primary result of which was a rapid growth in leisure time. This richness of leisure time suffered the inevitable perversion into a selfish, **radical individualism** as described by Charles Colson in his book, *The Body*.

The decades continued and are summarized as follows.

1940 – 1959	"Yes, Sir. I understand, Sir."
1960 - 1970	"Peace, Man, peace."
1971 - 1982	"Listen, who really cares?"
1983 - 1989	"Hey, Dude, chill out"
1990 - 1999	"It's mine, Baby, it's mine!"
2000 - ?	"I'll text you when I get there."

Somewhere in this chronology, radical visionaries (actually, reactionaries brave enough to be vocal) began what we now call the

Christian School Movement. Back to the academic basics, something called integration, short hair, classes started with prayer, and dress codes all became identifiable attributes of this exciting phenomenon.

First perceived as a non-Darwinian joke, the Christian School Movement slowly began forcing the public sector to consider change, at least publicly and politically. If you can't change the heart, at least you can put a cop in the corridor.

And finally, with the slow terror of a Poe-like pendulum, much of the Christian school movement is quietly acquiescing to the historical virus of mediocrity that has dulled the public sector. The safety of a dormant Christian status quo threatens to send this movement into the oblivion society reserves for the harmlessly eccentric.

Christian schools, secular private schools and Charter schools began to represent a serious threat to the government funded local schools. Teachers' Unions aggressively attacked any form of education threatening their monopoly on education, but a stronger, more effective counter began to lessen the impact of competitive education systems. The same creativity-killing syndrome turned many entrepreneurial ventures into mundane and boring businesses.

No longer new enough to be interesting nor radical enough to be exciting, a growing number of Christian schools are illustrating what I believe to be a foundational law that governs many societal institutions. I call this phenomenon the Law of Institutional Inertia.

Radical Ideas acted on with enthusiastic energy give rise to visionary institutions. Those institutions then tend to produce rules and structure designed to protect their own existence, thus stifling the production of further creative thought and radical ideas which created them in the first place.

There is a corollary law that applies to individuals.

Creative individuals who dare act on their creativity reach levels of success which become comfortable and secure, thus lessening the likelihood of further creative action.

The First Law of Motion as described by Isaac Newton discusses both the static and dynamic law of inertia. Both Institutional and Individual Inertia are static in nature. Creative ideas and enthusiastic energy allow an institution or person to reach a comfortable level of operation, but staying at that level eventually and inevitably turns a groove into the proverbial rut. That *rutism* can be avoided by choosing to live by the third law of Dynamic Institutional or Individual Inertia.

The willingness to risk failure...or the perception of failure... by fostering and acting on creative ideas is the only way to produce dynamic inertia and to develop a continuing and expanding acquisition of Radical Excellence.

To say it simply, be willing and anxious to enjoy the risk of becoming radically excellent.

Chap. 3 - Culture in Crisis

Hatred is something peculiar.
You will always find it strongest
and most violent where there is
the lowest degree of culture.

Johann Wolfgang von Goethe

DISCLAIMER: This chapter is most difficult, even scary, to write. It's scary because what I am about to discuss flies in the face of the chosen worldview of many people today. I suspect each of us has dealt with, or is currently dealing with. one or more of the issues that follow.

Open dialogue and true tolerance.

Political correctness and an unwarranted meaning of the word tolerance have resulted in a world of college "safe rooms," perceived micro-aggression and a growing epidemic of teenage "anxiety."

Words have meaning, but that meaning may vary based on geographical location, history and ethnicity. Hearing a trigger word for one person may induce a stress or emotion far-removed from the intent of the person saying the word.

Problems arise when the hearer of the word automatically assumes the user of the word intended it to be racist, sexist or critical. The user of the word then becomes a "Hater" and is considered intolerant.

Recently I observed a heated discussion between a transgender male and a straight male, both of whom had been good friends. The anger developed as the transgender male accused his former straight friend of being a Hater because the straight male was being "intolerant." By that, it appeared the transgender was equating disagreement with his chosen gender change as not being tolerant.

The straight male's response was totally correct.

"Look," he started. "The word *tolerant* means I can continue to accept you as my friend, even though I disagree with your worldview of gender identification. I do not hate you, even though I disagree with your viewpoint."

It is within that context I urge you to analyze the following ideas.

By the way, please understand. I do not write the following from a totally objective view. I have experienced directly or have had to deal with more than a couple of the ideas and concepts addressed.

Also, my intent in this book is not to produce an in-depth analysis of each of the following concepts. My goal is to simply propose these ideas contribute significantly to the current state of our culture and are worthy of open discussion about how education has been affected by these changes. Only then can we begin to develop strategies to help education improve.

Cultural Crisis #1: Darwin versus Design

Not long ago I walked into a faculty room lunch-time discussion about how best to teach Darwin's concept of natural selection to high school students. Ironically, one of my students had just asked an intriguing question.

I proceeded to ask the same question to my colleagues.

"How do you give a satisfactory answer to the fact that Darwinian Evolution does not align with the steps of the Scientific Method?"

The immediate response from one of the biology teachers at the table caught me off guard.

"I went to WalMart last night and got some great deals." was her *I-have-no-idea and I don't want to discuss it* response.

Sadly, most of the teaching of evolution comes only from the outdated textbooks often used. There is seldom any mention of modern evolutionary theories such as neutrality evolution or genome evolution. This lack of teaching more up-to-date theory illustrate a significant lack of scientific integrity, even within the totality of evolutionary theory.

More importantly, the unwillingness of many educational institutions to even discuss alternate concepts is more unscientific. Genuine science discussion will explore all plausible options before reaching conclusions based on substantive and logical support.

For instance, from the simplistic nature of a paperclip to the operational complexity of an airplane, it is undeniably obvious they were *DESIGNED*! Someone or a group of people decided to make them… and then developed the design into a product.

The problem is, the simplest of living things is remarkably more complex than the most complex of human-developed technology. Looking at the amazing structure and function of single-cell flagella motors or complex brain cell operations should automatically prompt the question, "How did this happen?"

Such questions, though they seldom occur, are simply dismissed as "given enough time," any complex system can be produced by evolutionary systems. This bail-out response is given without rational mechanism or observable facts.

Why, then, do we fear discussing the dichotomy between Evolutionary Theory and Intelligent Design?

Interestingly, the teaching of evolution coupled with the exclusion of any alternate model fits completely with the "having learned the NOT" concept addressed earlier in this book. What is left out is never learned.

"What is Left Out" teaches something

Furthermore, if we as humans are simply the current state of random molecular interactions, how can life possibly have purpose? If we are only a transitory stage, why should we worry about compassion, love, serving, poetry and morality? These are questions that desperately need to be addressed.

In my opinion the worst travesty of the evolutionary worldview is the lessening of the sanctity and worth of human life. And the absolutely worst result of that is the *Hidden Holocaust* resulting in the willful murder of millions of babies through abortion.

The continuous but subtle result of an evolutionary thesis is profound. If we as humans are a result of random molecular interactions, how is it possible for universal moral laws to exist?

Those who see abortion as a choice of ridding their body of simply cellular material have tried to redefine life as something fitting their convenience other than what life really is.

Ben Shapiro, a conservative talk-show host made an interesting point. He commented that if a single-cell that was living or once-living was found on Mars, headlines around the world would scream, "LIFE ON MARS." Yet the single cell human formed at conception is NOT considered life.

It's interesting how logic seems to vaporize when selfish motives conflict with fact.

Cultural Crisis #2: Addictions and Attitudes

A few years ago, my wife and I were visiting Yosemite National Park. Walking at the base of El Capitan we were overwhelmed and simultaneously inspired by the grandeur of this amazing feature.

About twenty-yards ahead, a young couple walked just a few feet in front of their young teen son. The animation and gestures of the couple reflected their own amazement.

Their son never once raised his eyes from the video game he was playing! His addiction to his device and game prevented any knowledge of the magnificence just thirty-yards to his right. To this day I regret not hastening my pace to be close enough to encourage the young man to simply look up!

Device addiction isn't limited to young teens. We have observed several instances of families in restaurants where each member of the family were focused on their device. Other times one person of a couple sits staring blindly into space as the other texts to someone else.

Other addictions still exist, as many have since recorded history.

- Drugs
- Alcohol
- Sex
- Pornography
- Social Media
- Mediocrity
- Apathy

The ultimate downside of any addiction is the mind-capture the addiction causes in the person. The addiction consumes their thoughts, thus diminishing creativity, analysis, thinking of productive ideas and even the appreciation of good puns or humor.

Cultural Crisis #3: Artificial Intelligence

Artificial Intelligence (AI) is exactly what the name says; computers and machines designed by people to take over tasks or procedures normally done by people. These tasks are often life-saving, work-reducing or simply enjoyment-creating events.

I battle an internal irony about the profound effect technology has on culture today. As a ninth-grader I became engrossed in amateur radio, building my own equipment and savoring interaction with other hams worldwide. My entire career and personal life has utilized various technologies almost on a daily basis.

There is some degree of sadness as I observe some of the negative changes caused by the increasing reliance on highly creative technological advances.

Take a look at just some of the items in our lives qualifying as AI.

- Directional Instructions by GPS apps on smartphones
- ATM machines or total banking apps
- Is Siri smarter than the homeowner?
- Lifelike robots as friends

- Endless automated phone instructions
- Easy-pay apps at gas stations and stores
- Online courses that tutor and grade work
- Robot controlled medical diagnosis and treatment
- Transhumanism and immortality (look it up… you will be mortified)
- Automatic spelling and grammar checking
- Voice to text apps and text to voice
- The "smart home" and "smart appliances"
- Smart Cars

That list barely taps the surface of AI involvement in our lives. Try this: for one week; keep a list of every single time you use or encounter something qualifying as Artificial Intelligence. Interestingly, the hardest part might prove to be actually recognizing the activity as AI. For instance, what about the traffic light that changes only when a vehicle is approaching from a given direction? Did you count that?

Please keep this in mind. Most things involving AI are legitimately classified as "good." They help us, they are beneficial individually and corporately.

The problem is quietly insidious. If our easy lives create a sense of dependence then when something unusual occurs, we may never have developed a sense of how to handle a difficult situation.

You see, one fact of an increasing dominance of Artificial Intelligence is **we no longer fix things.**

When I was about fourteen years old, our rotary dial phone stopped working. It made a quiet buzz, but the loud, attention getting ring was missing.

"Do you think you can fix it?" my mother asked with some degree of optimism in her question, likely because she had observed me building my amateur radio equipment. Living on a farm also contributed to the logic of repair since that's what farmers do… they fix things. Or at least they used to.

Using a Phillips screwdriver and my favorite needle-nose pliers I dismantled the device, adjusted a few screws and had the ring back again. Interestingly, I didn't have to spend twenty minutes selecting a new ringtone. What you had was what you got.

It's not that simple now.

If we can't fix a non-working electronic device by a software update or talking to the guy in India, we hope our two-year contract is up and we qualify for an upgrade. If that's the case, our life is stable again and we get on with texting, watching viral videos of cats, babies or the most recent "cop shoots kid" event.

Our old, hard-wired phones did only one thing; they made calls. They didn't tell us where we were, had no calculator or act as a camera or flashlight. They couldn't even hook up to Google... errrr... wait... Google hadn't been invented yet.

On the other hand, those old klunkers didn't spy on us, give out personal information to the bad guys or become an addictive EED. (Electronic Enjoyment Device)

The good, the bad and the ugly.

Whether being held Linus-blanket-like in our hands or hidden in the deep recesses of our car, smart devices have become the ubiquitous necessity of our age. As long as a cell tower is in electronic access, hikers no longer need to worry about moss on the northwest side of trees, travelers never have to meet interesting people who give verbal directions to the best diner in town or we never have to interpret body language or voice inflection as conversations are reduced to text-language acronyms.

Who really cares? Life is good, especially when Facebook allows us to share with all our electronic friends that we just went to Walmart and recognized the greeter as our next door neighbor. LOL!

Sometimes I wonder... maybe a good EMP would be a welcome event, forcing us to rekindle (pun intended) the skill of critical thinking.

And if you don't know what that last sentence means, there is always Google.

Cultural Crisis #4: Redefined Relationships

There was a time, not so long ago, when the concept of family meant one thing; a female mother, male father and boys or girls as kids. Of course, there were variations on that theme, but the implied norm was the traditional family.

The single most influential event resulting in massive change may have been World War II. Men went off to war and women went to work. It wasn't just that Mom was no longer at home raising kids. Now single women began choosing career over convention.

This transition is certainly not bad, but it did initiate a transition from tradition to a more independent and open life.

As life expectations and goals changed, those ideas and concepts long considered "normal" took on new meaning.

Twenty-first century living is now open and culturally accepting of a radical change in lifestyle.

Early in my teaching career the concept of a "melting pot" America meant the development of our country by the melding together of immigrants from many countries and customs.

The melting pot has become a cultural stew. In the latter part of my teaching career, it was no longer safe or wise to assume anything about the culture in which students lived.

A simple question, "What does your Dad think about this?" has the potential to be considered sexist, racist or politically incorrect.

Now, when students enter our classroom or show up on our socially distant screen, one or more of the following descriptors may be relevant.

Representative Terms of Family Groups

Nuclear family	Drug addicted	Homeless
Racially mixed	Alcoholic	Cult members
Gay	Working parents	Strict
Lesbian	Porn stars	Liberal
Divided	Enabling	Conservative
Divorced	Rich	Humanists
Abusive	Poor	Transgender
Illegals	Transients	Unemployed

Without question, these various groupings have always existed, and most importantly, co-existed without rancor and perceived hatred.

All that changed with the advent of identity culture and misuse of the word tolerance. At some point it became necessary to be known by a certain label. Not only known by that label, but others were expected to agree with the chosen lifestyle.

No longer was it possible to live harmoniously in a diverse community, but you were expected to agree with all others. Obviously there have always been those who aggressively disagreed with and treated others poorly. They were generally a minority and were opposed by people on both sides of any lifestyle.

This expected agreement with all lifestyles resulted in our next cultural crisis.

Cultural Crisis #5: The Death of Dialogue

In any context we should always be sensitive to how our words may affect others. Blatant disrespect or hurtful comments are never acceptable.

Problems arise when unwarranted and extreme perception interprets words as being disrespectful or demeaning even though the user of the word held neither of those attitudes. A lecturer describing an electrical engineer as "he" is not creating exclusivity nor is a textbook showing a picture of a woman nurse being stereotypical.

Over-reaction to words has created a subtle fear of speaking out on a subject. Who knows? The speaker might use a "politically incorrect" phrase that changes the intended dialogue to one of dissent over having offended the listener. The tendencies have thus become silence on one side or running off to a college-level "safe room" to cuddle a friendly Teddy Bear.

Whoops! Sorry. Teddy is likely sexist. Should have said "…to cuddle a *They* Bear."

This whole idea of political correctness has created a dynamic mix of conflicting attitudes and ideas.

Disagreement about ideas, philosophies or lifestyle choices do not make you a hater or intolerant. More importantly, disagreement does not prevent you from loving the one with whom you disagree. In fact, appropriately discussed disagreements help you become more insightful, analytical, maybe even creative.

Whether intended or not, political correctness has become a mechanism for defending weak ideas. If a person or group holds to an idea, philosophy or lifestyle which cannot be defended by logic or fact, one or more of the following occur.

- People or speakers with opposing views are shouted down
- Opposing views are ridiculed or laughed at derisively
- Protests by groups are held, preventing opposing events
- Those with opposing views are totally ignored or never reported on
- Derogatory terms like racist or bigot are rendered

Ironically, many of those who hold others to politically correct thinking have no problem with espousing openly contradictory statements or actions.

For instance, one state in which I taught openly said, "You are never to state your personal political view in the classroom." Then, in a mandatory workshop, teachers were informed it was now required to "mention specifically the gay lifestyle of selected scientists, poets, historians, etc."

Here is the real irony; to bring either of those issues up for public debate would have been considered unacceptable and adversarial.

For those willing to observe the society in which we live, the next crisis is obvious.

Cultural Crisis #6: Moral Relativism

"What's wrong with copying someone's homework? It doesn't hurt anybody." That sentence is heard on a regular basis by teachers who have uncovered blatant cheating.

One teacher discovered a supposedly original poem copied word for word from a famous author. The ***mother's*** words were astounding; "It's just a coincidence my daughter wrote those same words."

A student actually handed in an multi-page paper with only the title page his original work. The remaining pages were literally copy and pasted from online websites. When being confronted, the student's response was, "But I did the research and found all that stuff."

It isn't only school where moral integrity is compromised. We all are likely familiar with politicians who solicit our votes by promising certain actions when elected. Once in office their votes are contrary to those promises to gain favor with other politicians or external interest groups.

Society is replete with telephone and Internet scams, lying salesmen, shoplifting and a plethora of other misleading or totally false circumstances.

Even in the most fundamental of all decisions, the choice of a life-directing worldview is rationalized by saying, "It doesn't matter what you believe as long as you are serious about it."

How did we get to this awful place?

The re-writers of American history would do well to actually read the Declaration of Independence.

> "…When, in the course of human events, it becomes necessary for one people to dissolve the political bonds which have connected them with another, and to assume among the powers of the earth, the separate and equal station to which the laws of nature and of nature's God entitle them, a decent respect to the opinions of mankind requires that they should declare the causes which impel them to the separation.
>
> We hold these truths to be self-evident, that all men are created equal, that they are endowed by their Creator with certain unalienable rights, that among these are life, liberty and the pursuit of happiness…"

I graduated from high school in 1959. That was the year the original lawsuit was filed to ban the following from public schools.

> *"Almighty God, we acknowledge our dependence on Thee, and
> we beg Thy blessings upon us, our parents, our teachers and our
> country."*

We recited that prayer together immediately after saying the pledge to the American flag.

> *"I pledge allegiance to the Flag of the United States of America,
> and to the Republic for which it stands, one Nation under God,
> indivisible, with liberty and justice for all."*

The important point of the preceding quotes isn't only the mention of a God-Creator, but also the inference a standard existed. Concepts of right and wrong do exist, regardless of those who promote the false narrative of revisionist history.

The problem, however, isn't just the continuing false narrative. The reality is that many in the general population have no comprehension of the significance of our historical documents and the principles on which they were founded. That fatal ignorance, in my opinion, is the systemic failure of our educational system.

I posit that moral relativism is the expected result of a combination of evolutionary thinking, political correctness, the attempt at philosophical inclusion and the misinterpretation of the concept of tolerance.

Parents know that what isn't taught almost always results in the opposite of the missing lesson. If a child is never taught about sharing, the ultimate selfishness of "mine" becomes the acquired lesson.

Similarly, if public schools never really teach the character values illustrated in the Judeo-Christian tradition on which our nation is based, the only logical learned lesson is that moral relativism is the accepted worldview.

Part 2 - *America, we have a solution.*

The problem faced by the Apollo 13 crew needed to be solved. Anything short of a functional fix was fatal. Plus, it could only be solved by materials and devices on board the spacecraft.

NASA leadership wisely initiated the remedy immediately, but equally wisely, placed the process in the hands of the engineers and technicians who designed and built the craft.

Working quickly and efficiently, grassroots experts initiated a plan using common material and creative ideas to fix the problem and bring the crew back to earth safely.

People are the Promise

Inherent problems permeate education, and the result will be a cultural fatality if those difficulties are not solved swiftly and efficiently.

Educational leadership has demonstrated continuing failure in solving the problem. From governmental to administrative hierarchy, the students leaving the educational system through graduation or dropping out still exhibit an unacceptable level of thinking, analyzing and creating in a rapidly deteriorating culture.

It is time for us, the grassroots people, to speak up, stand up and stand out as we use what is available to start a cultural revolution designed to bring our nation back to its historical foundations.

Part 2 focuses on three groups of people who need to join forces as we enter the revolutionary phase of educational renewal.

- Parents
- Students
- All of us

Teachers are not omitted from the list, but included in the "all" section. Teachers and administrators will be addressed in Part 3.

Please note, much of the following three chapters are condensations and moderate revisions of three of my previous ebooks; *A+ Parenting, Get a Grip – Join life* and *Live Better from the Inside Out.*

Chap. 4 - Twenty-First Century Parenting

Who Knew?

Parenting changes everything, doesn't it?

That softly crying babe in the delivery room now comes home from fourth grade with math homework... or maybe that little babe is now sixteen and still not back with the car he's driving for the first time.

Maybe it's the boys. They're always texting your daughter, asking her for help on homework, or so she says.

Speaking of homework, you are convinced your child did it right, and the grade would be higher than the "D" in biology.

The twenty-first century brings some unique difficulties into the process of raising good kids.

- An abundance ofElectron ic Entertainment Devices
- Instant communication with friends by texting and cellphone
- Communication with you decreasing
- The trauma of being a single parent
- TV, online streaming and movies that constantly push the moral envelope
- Increasing prevalence of ADHD and anxiety
- The continuing difficulty of undiagnosed dyslexia (processing problems)
- Government enforced "stay at home" school

It is not easy being a twenty-first century parent, but there are guiding principles that can help you get started or stay on the road to success and a good life for your child.

Focus on Hope

Thomas Jefferson

We are all aware of the obvious... school should make sense and be a successful experience for your child.

It doesn't take a brilliant mind to understand that principle, but we sometimes forget exactly what it is that makes school success possible for your child.

First of all, your child's success in school goes far beyond the grade they achieve in any particular class or how well they do on the infamous standardized exams. Doing well with grades or on standardized tests is a **byproduct** of students choosing to follow the pursuit of a concept that I call HOPE.

In this case, HOPE is an acronym meaning **"Higher Order Principles of Education."**

Simply stated, it is important to live by those Higher Order Principles of Education. We and our students must live by actively applying normal, traditional values to whatever we do.

The Journey To Radical Excellence.

If your children make a focused effort towards living their lives within the context of those Higher Order Principles, they will ultimately produce a life that excitingly illustrates a high level of Radical Excellence.

You need to understand this; these Higher Order Principles of Education are not matters of lifestyle choices. Rather, they are universally accepted concepts which have been traditionally considered as logical, positive characteristics. I do acknowledge there are certain groups who consider these characteristics as racist. That statement is so illogical I dismiss it as totally absurd.

Some of those "traditional values" are listed here.

> Responsibility
> Enthusiasm
> Integrity
> Curiosity
> Politeness
> Timeliness
> Commitment
> Politeness

The danger in saying those things is that people will think, "Well of course! We all know that."

Most of us DO know those things, but here's a disturbing fact. When those characteristics are not reaffirmed continuously they quietly disappear from culture, and the norm becomes a self-oriented "do my own thing" lifestyle.

EED's… the roadblock to success.

More and more in our schools, public or private, a growing number of students have become enjoyably engrossed in their use of Electronic Enjoyment Devices to the extent they are forgetting (or ignoring) the productive application of those excellence-producing characteristics.

Saying something and actually doing that thing is what makes a hoped-for success possible. Genuine beliefs are illustrated by what a person does, not what they say. Saying, "I know I spend too much time texting." yet continue making several thousand text a month sends the actual belief of the person.

Having stated those principles used in producing excellent achievement, I would be guilty of a great omission if I didn't give you a practical examples of a specific activity you can do that will help your child in school.

Ask the right questions.

A typical dinner time conversation with your teenage child might sound like this.

"How was school today?"

"OK."

"Is all your homework done?"

"Yeah."

You might be amazed at the dialogue that could develop simply by changing the way you ask questions of your child. Let me give you a few examples.

"What was the funniest thing any of your teachers said today?"

"What questions did you ask in class today?"

"Which of your friends was the most enjoyable to be around?"

"Did you observe any acts of random kindness?"

"Let's study those vocabulary terms right after dinner, ok?"

"How did your math teacher help you see where math is used in everyday life?"

"Are you getting used to working online?"

"Is it easier or harder to stay focused with the online learning?"

At the beginning of each school year we hear multitudes of inspirational words about how "We're all in this together."

Well, the fact is, we ARE in it together.

Let's see if we can make it work.

The Blame Game

You can get discouraged many times,
but you are not a failure
until you begin to blame somebody else and stop trying."

John Burroughs

There are times when life isn't any fun.

The problem times of life can arise from an abundance of reasons, and when we are dealing with those times, we tend to place blame on someone else or some remote situation.

Whose fault is it?

The pervasive and undefined *society* is always an easy target.

Reading the morning paper or seeing the news headlines online frequently creates the response, "What is our society coming to, anyway?"

Blaming society, seemingly absolves us from personal involvement in a stressful situation. If society is the fundamental cause of the problems we face, who are we to think it possible to stand up and personally attack a problem? How can one individual make a difference?

Next in line to take the brunt of determining what causes a child's poor performance at school is the *neighborhood*. Where you live might not be the best place in the world, and certainly there are deficiencies that could have great influence on your kids. Significant poverty, an abundance of gang-bangers and massive unemployment are all major factors that do affect how we live.

On the other hand, you and your family can become victorious over anything if you go about it in the right way.

You need to be strong. Be patient. Dig deep and develop the courage to become victors over tough circumstances.

The electronic universe.

I call them EED's (*Electronic Enjoyment Devices*), and the all-encompassing presence of smartphones, video games and computers is another focus where we can place blame for the shortcomings of our children. When you see thousands of text messages per month on your phone bill, maybe it's time to quit blaming the device. Rather than the device, the real problem resides with the decision-making ability of your child, or perhaps, your own unwillingness to curtail your child's cellphone account.

When the school report card comes home with two D's and one F and the rest C's, you may hear the common lament, "Everybody's doing poorly in those classes. The teachers really don't care about us and are not good at all."

Understand one simple fact when you hear the phrase "everybody is doing poorly" being translated usually means, "my three friends and I have the lowest grades in the class."

If you aren't perceptive and persistent, it is easy to fall into the trap of blaming *teachers* for your child's poor academic performance. There are times when your child may actually have a poor teacher, but almost always there are flaws in the daily routine of the student that result in their poor performance.

If it isn't teachers, the negatives in your child can always be blamed on their *friends*. If they only hung out with better kids, they would have better habits and thus do better in school. Peer pressure is a genuinely strong factor and definitely has an effect on the habits and attitudes of our children. That pressure can be positive, but mostly seems to dwell on the negative.

As parents, we can quickly fall into the syndrome of blaming *drugs* for the poor performance of our children. The insidious danger of drugs cannot be ignored, but we must never fall into the trap of ascribing blame for the failings of our children on drugs alone.

Blame might not be the cause.

All of the above reasons for blaming the factors that create deficiencies in our children might hide the real cause of their problems. This may be a hard thing to face, but the root of their problems might reside in the way your parenting has progressed… or not progressed.

As you continue through this book, I will suggest some very practical steps you can take that can result in improving the performance of your child in school. And as success in school becomes more apparent, the likelihood of success in other parts of their lives will increase.

For starters, you need to understand the starting point is realizing **The Mind Matters Most**. Every action, every decision starts with our minds. Everything we do is determined by what we think in our minds. From the smallest, most inconsequential items to major life-changing decisions, what we think in our mind ultimately determines the decisions we make.

Understand this. The decisions you make are yours. You need to own them, to take responsibility for the decision and the consequences of that decision.

Equally important, your children make their own decisions. You may try desperately to influence those decisions, but ultimately, they are the one who decide the actions that affect their lives.

Knowing this, there is only one logical conclusion.

Good parenting must focus on teaching our kids how to make wise decisions.

That is an easy statement to say, but not so easy to bring to fruition in daily living. Teaching good decision making requires patience, perception and most of all, wisdom.

The first practical step is to start early. A two year old's tantrum rewarded by giving in to their demands establishes a system where inappropriate actions get their selfish desires. Being patient and letting the tantrum end teaches the lesson you desire.

Children learn exceptionally fast during those early years, and your patient actions early on can result in a much more peaceful life later.

Enable or Empower?

It's not what happens to you,
but how you react to it that matters.

Epictetus

Just like there are no perfect parents, there are no perfect kids. Plan on it. Your perfect angel will get in trouble, whether at home or in school.

Dealing with imperfection.

When problems happen, how are you going to react? Will you be the parent who automatically sticks up for your child who would "never do that?" Will you be the great enabler, doing everything possible to make the problem go away?

Or will you choose to be the wise parent who tells their child, "You deserve the consequences you are facing. We won't help get you out of the problem, but we will help you through it."

That is an excellent support system. When you acknowledge the wrong, but provide the support to help your child survive and grow, you are teaching positive lessons rather than simply inflicting punishment.

Simply put... get it on - get it done - get over it.

Done properly, there are times where "enabling" is an acceptable alternative. Done poorly, however, the enabling situation can have detrimental effects. For instance, some teachers offer extra credit. Some students who ask for that extra credit are really asking for "bail me out" credit since they haven't done their part. Wise teachers can offer a form of credit recovery that still forces the student to suffer the appropriate degree of consequence.

Extra credit that fails to provide realistic consequences does little to help the student stay in touch with the reality of responsibility. One of the most absurd instances I have seen was the student whose grade went from an "F" to passing by accomplishing the "extra credit" of not shaving for the month of November. Somehow that doesn't seem to meet the criteria of turning the situation into a positive, learning situation.

Identify the real problem.

Enabling a student can also hide the real problem. If a poor grade in school is caused by a student being disorganized, but the fixing is accomplished by giving a re-test, nothing much is accomplished except teaching the student there is always a way out of the problem. The more appropriate "consequence" might be letting the grade stand, then teaching your child better organizational skills.

I had a student who received an "F" on a lab report because all the physics was totally wrong. His father called me, rather adamant that the failing grade was unfair because the student had "worked really hard." The father thought it entirely appropriate that hard work was far more important than correct performance on any graded event. The irony of that argument became apparent when I reminded the man that his clients (he was a contractor) would not likely be content with working hard if the roof he installed fell down after the first month.

I do understand why parents want to reward their children for "working hard," but it is much better to couple that positive life-attribute with the production of quality, not necessarily perfect, work.

What about cheating?

Perhaps the worst of all situations for enabling to occur is in the realm of cheating. None of us want to think our child would ever do such a thing, but the hard reality is that every kid is capable of giving in to that temptation. In those types of situations, no matter what the consequences, remember the bigger lesson of learning integrity far transcends any grade penalty the child might receive.

Your child's perception of you as a parent is at risk if you excuse their cheating or attempt to nullify the normal consequences. Your own actions will be perceived as lacking integrity, thus enhancing the rightness of the action, but also lessening the respect you are given.

High tech cheating has expanded the base of participants, and your child can become part of a cheating situation, even without the intent to do so. All it takes is one cheater with a cellphone and the contents of an exam can be known throughout their friends in the electronic universe.

All passengers in a car are guilty when one rider lights up a joint. The same is true and the guilt shared when the contents of a pilfered exam are sent out electronically.

School administrators have almost no choice but to count all recipients of a compromised exam guilty. Thus, a punishment could be applied to a large group of "friends," and your son or daughter could be included, even if they never used the material.

Your child will undoubtedly deny any involvement, and will most likely deny or defend the person who initiated the action. The "I would never rat on a friend" syndrome is very real, even if it is misdirected.

Never mentioning the event makes some degree of guilt a strong likelihood. When that happens, the proper thing to do is support whatever consequences the administrators propose – within reason.

The lesson learned here is to choose friends wisely and then inform someone, even parents, when inappropriate actions are occurring.

If your child is part of the cheating, it might also be a time to impose your own consequences in addition to those applied by the school. The school's punishment is for the cheating. Yours' is the violation of trust and integrity your child showed towards the family.

Reward or Punish?

If people are good only because they fear punishment,
and hope for reward, then we are a sorry lot indeed.

Albert Einstein

The student was quite irate when she approached my desk.

"You just cost me two-hundred dollars!" were her opening words.

She went on to explain in a rather animated and angry way that because I GAVE her a C in chemistry, the money her parents had promised for getting nothing less than a B was gone.

My explaining that her average was right in the middle of the "C" range did little to calm her spirit. Neither did she feel better when I indicated how proud I was that she had raised her first semester grade from a "D" to the "C."

After she calmed down, and the realization that I was not going to raise her grade set in, we began discussing some negotiation options with her parents. Interestingly, when she returned to school the next day, she was fairly satisfied because her parents understood the improvement was significant, and they had taken her suggestion to keep on trying for the "B," and to lower the reward to one-hundred-fifty dollars.

I have mixed feelings on the use of rewards of that magnitude for getting arbitrary grades in classes. It can illustrate the good news - bad news syndrome. It can be good news if it actually works, but it can be bad news if the child begins to believe that life is always like this.

The totally opposite approach can produce similar conflicts.

I have seen students be grounded for a month, had their car keys locked up or, worse yet, had their cellphone confiscated for getting less than acceptable grades.

Every student and family situation is different. Even children in the same family need to be treated differently at times. I admit to having mixed reactions to this style of reward or punishment. As a self-confessed idealist, I like emphasizing the Higher Order reasons for learning should take predominance over artificial rewards or punishment. Combining artificial grades to extrinsic rewards or punishment could dilute the learning and development of effective systems of doing the right thing in the right way.

One way of producing an effective compromise might be for the parent to give a partial reward for following a good system (i.e. doing the homework on time) while also rewarding the actual result.

Being a parent has never been easy. And today, I believe it has never been harder. Never has it been more critical to establish open lines of communication with your kids.

Start early, never give up. Your kids are your legacy. Make it good.

Reading Really Works

You don't have to burn books to destroy a culture.
just get people to stop reading them.

Ray Bradbury

The more that you read, the more things you will know.
The more that you learn, the more places you'll go.

Dr. Seuss, *I Can Read With My Eyes Shut!*

Even in this digital video age, reading is still the fundamental skill that we all need. And we are not talking the banal travesty we call texting, either. Genuine reading, whether for enjoyment or information, is an absolute necessity.

As a parent who wants your child to succeed, there are several undeniably important facts you must comprehend and illustrate. Some of them might be things you already know. Other could be ideas worth trying as you help your child achieve real academic success.

Success will be more likely for your child if they see you modeling the joy and functionality of reading. Kids do emulate their parents, and it is way more functional to say "Here, try doing this. It works for me." than to tell them to do something that you NEVER do.

Another critical component is to start the process early. Early in their lives, during those pre-bedtime snuggle moments, start with a colorful picture book. The sound of your voice, the warmth of your hugs and the presence of a book create a positive environment that gives confidence and joy to your child.

I said it before, but it needs repeating. You absolutely must be convinced that the ability to read for enjoyment and understanding is one of the most critical components of success in almost all endeavors of life. It cannot be ignored. It must be pursued.

You likely have already provided your child with their own cellphone. Serious consideration should be given to making their own ebook reader available. I still enjoy the tactile comfort of a traditional book, but the ownership of a reading device of their own emphasizes the importance of reading.

A positive family atmosphere can occur that emphasizes good reading by all reading the same novel, then sharing reactions and comments about it while eating the evening meal together.

You heard that right, didn't you?

Eating the evening meal TOGETHER is becoming a lost tradition, but I am convinced of the long-term benefit of sharing time and nutrition as a family.

Family reading does not need to be formalized, but by selected discussions, it is possible to develop useful academic skills necessary for school success.

Thinking, analyzing, comparing and summarizing can all be emphasized by appropriate questioning and discussing?

Start early, stay the course, and think of the joy you will have as a grandparent discussing great books with your kids.

Safe Surfing

The Internet is so big, so powerful and pointless
that for some people it is a complete substitute for life

Andrew Brown

Surfing the web is potentially more dangerous than riding a monster wave off the California coast. Who knows what evil lurks in that electronic abyss so easily accessed by our smart devices. The real danger of sexual predators or identity thieves can ruin lives in a moment.

Equally dangerous is the mental dullness and insensitivity to reality that can develop as your children live in this virtual world of weird videos and imagined demons. It is highly unlikely that unlimited texting or tweeting produces well-thought-out writing or discussion of deeply philosophical ideas.

The oxymoronic nature of the Internet is that with all its distractions and potential evils, there has never existed a medium more conducive to in-depth research, highly creative products and even the potential to provide service to others and profit to individuals.

There is a real battle in progress as the easy entertainment duels with the productive potential of the Internet and our amazingly brilliant machines. Unfortunately, as the machines tend to get "smarter," the users can become dumber.

It is our job as parents to help guide our kids on a path to develop the desire and skills in using what is at their fingertips for an ally rather than a destructive force. We need to show them that the Internet is more than online games and that research is more than an online encyclopedia.

Common Sense Media indicates teens spend an average of nine hours per day online or on their devices. Kids eight to twelve spend six hours per day. Think about it; that's a full day of work and a full week of work plus overtime. Not only are there negative results from the online activity itself, but the time spent NOT doing other productive activities can remove many wonderful experiences from your child.

Positive Practical Protections

There are some simple actions you can do to help keep your kids safe and focused.

- Install a content blocker on their computer
- Check the history of their computer use frequently.
- Place the family computer in a visible location.
- Set a limit on the number of texts sent per month.
- Become a "friend" on your child's social networks.
- Set a limit on the number of texts per month
- Check the time when texts are sent
- Determine the amount of time spent texting per month

then require an equivalent amount of time be spent reading

Some Positive Family Actions

It is not all negative, and there are many positive things you can do as a family in using the Internet.

- Play online thinking games like chess or word games
- Make family videos and upload them to YouTube
- Build a computer controlled robot
- Learn to use "voice to text" for writing school papers
- Learn how to write and publish an ebook together
- Start a family Internet business
- Learn how to do geocaching… then do it.
- Start a family blog

The real key is to start doing family activities. Quit using "I don't have time" excuses. If you don't have time for your family you absolutely need to revisit your priority list.

Nothing Happens by Accident

Everything is a choice.

Remember, ***the mind matters most***.

Left to their own decision making process, it seems that most kids will somehow tend to make negative decisions. Your role as a parent is to model wise choices in your own personal use of modern technology and guide, even control, the Internet use by your children.

Just as proper driving technique is a learned and developed skill, the same is true of computer use. Left on their own to become adept at driving a car, you can expect a wreck from your child. Do all you can to prevent a mental or emotional wreck in the world of using the Internet or smartphones.

The Risk of Trying

I can accept failure,
everyone fails at something.
But I can't accept not trying.

Michael Jordan

A growing syndrome in classrooms is the student who sits in class and does nothing except breathe and grow older. And *nothing* means exactly that... nothing! Often the same is true for that student in other situations; watching TV, playing video games and doing nothing productive towards school or building a better life.

The results are obvious.

Do nothing - get terrible grades.

Do nothing – increase apathy and mediocrity

When exams or papers are returned, the response is still nothing. No overt sign of disappointment or positive resolve is apparent, just a continuing attitude of nothing.

In my opinion, there is an underlying event occurring. If a student doesn't do homework, never studies and is only consistent in doing nothing, there is automatically a possible response.

"If I had studied, I would have passed." is their inner response to terrible grades.

By **not** studying, the student can hold firmly to the false optimism of, "If only..."

If they DO study, and still get a bad grade, their poor performance becomes internally personal and they are forced to confront other issues.

This syndrome may have been initiated by poor prior performance that was never addressed or cured.

Be careful in your parenting here. Overly negative criticism about a problem can lead to giving up. When criticizing a situation try and give positive support and suggestions on being successful.

Start trying. It might actually work.

If you sense your child might be slipping into this attitude of nothingness, or is already there, you can take definitive action to reverse the trend.

- Know the problem will not be solved immediately.
- Time management skills may need to be improved.
- You may have to impose scheduled homework times.
- You may need to teach organizational skills.
- A tutor can provide incentive to start trying again.

This will not cure itself.

Unfortunately, this type of activity (or inactivity) seldom fixes itself. It is a self-perpetuating syndrome that becomes addictive, and can lead to forms of depression. The student who is doing nothing wishes internally for the energy and ambition to try and do the right thing, but is unable to generate the incentive to change.

That is where you as a parent enter the picture. It may require highly directive action or, depending on the actual circumstances, more of a gentle, counseling approach.

Speaking of counseling, there are times where extreme inaction or withdrawal of energy may be the result of some type of trauma in the child's life. Divorce, drugs or the death of a family member or friend can trigger emotions and feelings that prevent the person from performing as they know they should.

Be alert to your child. You need to have the wisdom to take action when and where it is obviously needed.

Count Your Pills

With significant drug use starting as early as middle school, it is critical that you are aware of the symptoms of drug use. Those symptoms can appear as normal middle school changes or activities, but you should be alert to what might be going on in your child's life.

Some symptoms of marijuana use.

Marijuana is readily available in almost any neighborhood or school. Its use can affect behavior and there are also some physical signs of its use.

Become alert if your child is showing some of the following symptoms. Is your child showing…

- Lack of motivation, even on former enjoyment?
- Decreasing participation in former groups?
- Slow or rapid decline in school performance?
- Not wanting to engage in family activities?
- A sudden change in peer group?
- Decrease in appearance or hygiene ?
- Symptoms of depression?
- Sudden increase in aggressive behavior?

Marijuana use, unlike alcohol, where the signs of use are often overt and overwhelming, is not always easy to detect. There are some physical signs that should make you suspicious that your child might be using marijuana.

- Bloodshot eyes
- Slow or slurred speech
- Lack of eye contact or unfocused gaze
- Unusual shower times to minimize smell
- Unusual use of eye drops to clear bloodshot eyes.

Even though there is a strong push towards the legalization of marijuana, it is still considered by many to be a "gateway" to harder, more dangerous drugs. Please understand that legalization of marijuana will not lessen the potential dangers inherent in its use. You must continue to be vigilant and proactive in preventing your child from using marijuana either recreationally or as a reality escape.

Harder drugs can cause more extreme symptoms, some of which are listed below. Those listed come from the website http://drugs.ie/drugs_info/ and a more exhaustive list can be found on their site.

Important signs and symptoms of hard drug use.

There are some general signs to watch out for which may be linked to drug use. Bear in mind that all of the signs listed below could be caused by many reasons other than drug use such as puberty, social changes or medical conditions. Try not to jump to conclusions about drug use, as you may be wrong and isolate your teenager even more.

- Secrecy about activities, slyness, caginess
- Staying out unusually late
- A lot of new friends, perhaps an older crowd
- Lack of interest in old hobbies and activities
- Memory loss
- Mood swings – including fits of temper
- Short attention span
- Not taking care of their appearance
- Using unglasses to hide effects of drugs on the eyes
- Using deodorant or incense to hide the smell of drugs
- Always being broke and trying to borrow money

- Stealing from home or outside
- Using slang terms for drugs
- Social, personal and family relationships suffer
- Poor work or school skipping
- Losing appetite and weight
- Becoming withdrawn and not wanting to talk

Check Your Medicine Cabinet

It is not easy being a parent. From all sides you are bombarded by messages from different groups; should you spank your child or not? Should Mom work or stay home? Attend public school or private. Couple those pressures with an increasing governmental involvement, and parenting successfully is becoming complicated.

There is one issue that is very straight forward. Or at least it should be.

Our kids should not be using drugs. But even in this issue there are levels of grayness.

For instance, some parents are either indifferent towards or blind about the misuse of prescription drugs by their children. In fact, some even think it is safe for a child to use a prescription drug not prescribed to them, either recreationally or for self-medicating illness or "not feeling well."

Ominous Findings

There are some scary findings from a study recently conducted by The Partnership at Drugfree.org that indicate an unexpected casual approach by many parents regarding the use and misuse of prescription drugs.

One in four teens has misused prescription drugs.

Prescription drug abuse has increased 33 percent since 2008.

Only 15 percent of parents talk to their children about misusing prescription drugs.

20 percent of teens were under 14 years old when they first tried drugs.

The most commonly abused prescription drugs are Xanax, OxyContin and Vicodin.

Those drugs cause more deaths per year than heroin and cocaine combined.

Some parents and many kids think abusing prescription stimulants will help get good grades.

Almost one-third of parents believe that Ritalin and Adderall can help a child perform better academically.

One in four teens believes prescription drugs aid in study.

What steps can you take?

There are some proactive steps you can take to help your child make wise decisions about prescription drugs.

- Talk with your child, starting early, about the dangers of prescription drugs.
- Spend time with your child to keep their respect and to maintain good communication.
- Keep close watch on your prescription medications and dispose of unused medications promptly and properly.
- Model proper behavior about prescription drugs.
- Listen carefully to their words.

At Home Alcohol Abuse

One of the more subtle substance abuse areas for teens can be the in-home bar area. A small drink here, another there, and your child may be starting down the road towards dependence on alcohol.

If you do have a bar or wine cellar, it is wise to keep a close eye on the remaining amounts. If you have younger children who might not have the wisdom or knowledge to try small amounts, it may even be a good idea to keep your liquor cabinet locked. A small body and too much alcohol can be a deadly combination.

Another danger signal for the potential misuse of alcohol is if your fifteen or sixteen year old teen is suddenly hanging out with similar age friends, but with a twenty-one-year old in the group. That is the one who could legally purchase the alcohol, then make it available to the group.

Amazingly, there are also parents who provide alcohol to underage teens when a party is being held at their home. Any rumors or allegations that you hear about such activities should wave a red flag boldly in your face, and should be totally investigated before letting your teen attend a party in such a place.

Find where to get help.

If your child is misusing any substances at all, you may find that eliminating the problem is beyond your personal ability to solve. In that case, it is your responsibility as a parent to seek outside help, whether professionally or not.

The most important issue here is to let go of the need for total privacy. It may be embarrassing or you may even feel like a parental failure, but the health and welfare of your child is more important than temporary discomfort on your part.

There are some logical first steps to take.

- Perhaps you have friends who have gone through similar problems. Start there.
- Counselors at your child's school might be able to provide insight.
- Your church may have a support or intervention program.
- It may be necessary to seek the help of professional substance abuse workers.
- If extreme intervention is necessary, some sort of rehab or intervention may be required.

Start Early. Never Give Up.

This has been a long section, but substance abuse is a big problem. Often it is a problem we are blind to until it becomes extreme. It is also one we sometimes do not want to face.

"Not my child..." is a safety barrier many parents erect. They ignore the problem until their child is in serious, perhaps deadly, circumstances.

You are not infringing on your child's privacy if you are alert and proactive in keeping them free from substance abuse. Indeed, it is your responsibility to do so. That intervention or

Investigation may create tense, even adversarial, moments. Those will not be enjoyable times, but the benefit will eventually overcome the distress of those times.

Do not ignore the obvious. Intervene. Seek help. Be successful.

Learn Their Language

I would make an anonymous call and say,
this is someone who cares,
do you know what kind of children you have?

Elizabeth Berg, *Joy School*

Words are important. So are the words hidden between the lines or shown in the body. And with the increasingly hidden life of many teenagers, the current meanings of words can carry disastrous messages.

It is not just the unique abbreviations used in texting (lol, bff, etc.) but the spoken words that convey a message expected to be hidden from parents and older people... meaning anyone over thirty.

For instance, the phrase, "go nike..." sends a message of sexual activity. As you remember, the Nike corporation had an advertising campaign that said, "just do it!" Many teens have taken that phrase, changed it to "go nike," meaning just do it... meaning let's have sex.

FWB is a shorthand notation meaning "Friends With Benefits." Those benefits can include a broad spectrum, but mostly focused on either sexual activity or drug use.

Kids are not stupid, but they think we are.

Any kid dumb enough to be talking on their cellphone in your presence and use the word marijuana or heroin is too dumb to not have been caught already. They will use one or more of the common street names for the various drugs.

For instance, if you hear the numbers 420 slipped into a conversation you can be sure they are not telling the time of the party. 420 is simply one of the more common street names for marijuana.

If you listen carefully to what your kids are saying, you might not have a clue what they are talking about. Teen slang is constantly changing, and some of the meanings of common sounding phrases would surprise, maybe even shock you. The word meaning one thing today can change almost instantly into a totally different meaning, or a brand new slang term can appear suddenly in your child's vocabulary.

Following is a short list of some of the more common slang terms.

1. *Chillin'* - Means relaxing.

2. *Dope* - Means cool or awesome.

3. *Fly* - Boys tend to refer to girls they think are good looking as 'fly'.

4. *Hater or h8er* - This refers to someone who hates everything.

5. *Hardcore* - Means something is intense, generally good, but not always so.

6. *My bad* - It means 'my mistake'.

7. *OMG* - An abbreviation for oh my gosh or oh my god!

8. *Sick*- This no longer means someone doesn't feel well. It is used to describe something or someone who is cool or awesome.

9. *Tight* - Means close in relationship, as in "Me and her are tight." Note the generally wrong use of pronouns by teens.

10. *Tool* - A person who is either stupid or a geek.

11. *Wanksta* - A person who trys to act tough, but isn't successful at it.

One of the most complete compilations of teen slang can be found at http://www.thesource4ym.com/SlangDictionary/SlangDictionary.aspx

CAUTION: the above list was compiled in 2019. You should do an Internet search to see what's happening today.

Body language speaks louder.

When body language does not line up with the words your child is saying, you must use great wisdom in how you respond. You know what they say is definitely not the truth or what they really think, but almost always an adversarial response will only deepen the problem.

"Don't roll your eyes at me." might not be the best way to confront the message they are sending. Rather, you will be wise to incorporate their body language logically into the conversation.

Try a response like, "I know you are frustrated, but try and see it from my perspective, even a little bit." You may find that response will enable the conversation to continue in a more fruitful manner.

Know Their Friends

Rebecah McManus, *Colliding Worlds*

Kids jump first!

We know wisdom arrives after experience, and the choice of friends our children make is a classic example. A vibrant and authoritative personality can suck our offspring into an intriguing relationship that can be either good, bad or really ugly.

The importance of information.

Knowing who your child hangs out with is critical to their success and safety. The proper friends can have positive results, while choosing in a bad way can lead your child down a path that could take years, even a lifetime, to recover from.

You need to set the tone early that you want to know who their friends are, and what kind of people they happen to be. Parental responsibility mandates that you have that information, and, especially when your child is younger, can determine who their primary friends are.

Friends are crucial in the bringing up of children. Real friends, not electronic images on flat screens, but friends who get together and go bowling, join in neighborhood activities, maybe even have "study for test" parties.

It might not be comfortable, but keeping close track of your child's friends is important. There are some definitive actions you can do to give you the information needed. Most importantly, start early in the process and the intervention you are exerting will be natural and expected as your child grows into the teenage years.

- If your house allows it, try and host parties and provide a place for small groups of friends to hang out together.

- When that is not possible, make sure you know what the parents who are hosting are like. Do you have confidence the hosting parents would conduct the party in a way that makes you comfortable?

- If your child says they are going to a party at a particular place, it is totally okay to make a call or visit just to make sure what you were told is actually happening.

- There may be opportunity to ask your child's teachers or counselors what kind of friends your child has at school, and whether the teacher thinks they are wise choices.

- Join an athletic team and participate as a family.

- Find things your family and other friends with kids of similar age can do together.

Check technological friends.

In our keyboard-connection world, you need to keep a close watch on your child's online and texting friends. Just as with the living and breathing friends, there are things you can do to help your child make proper decisions.

- Always be a member of their social media adventures.

- Make it a habit to check their smart phone address book.

- Br sure you have passwords for email and other accounts your child uses.

- Check the cellphone texting use. Make sure it lines up with what you see on their phone.

- In extreme cases, you may find it necessary to install tracking devices on your automobile if used by your teenage driver.

This is the 21st Century!

Times are not like when you were a kid. Mostly, thing are better and enjoyment is more easily obtained. The nuclear family differs remarkably from what you experienced growing up. Technology has made "friendships" possible without ever meeting face-to-face... until a disaster could occur.

Thus, even though you may be uncomfortable and feel like you are spying on your kids, it has now become an acceptable and necessary component of parenting. So buck it up. Know your child... and his or her friends.

But my child has NO friends.

If your child has no friends and is a total "loaner," that could be indicative of a potentially dangerous situation. You may need to create situations in which interaction with others is possible. Chances are your child is uncomfortable with meeting new peers, and it then becomes your job as a parent to find safe situations in which friendships can be developed slowly and within the comfort level of your child.

You can do that by having your child join small, safe groups at church or community groups in which you also participate. Even participating in a 5k benefit walk can start the interacting with others.

On the negative side, if your son or daughter is friendless, that may be a symptom of a deeper problem. In that case, seeking the aid of a counselor or professional could be the wisest action you can take.

There are no easy answers to the skill of raising good kids. The process requires the knowledge and wisdom to determine whether to intervene or not. You want to raise your children to be independent, yet to havBut those interventions and modeling occur at a young age will, more often than not, create confidence and growing wisdom in your teenage children.

Be strong.
Be patient.
Be a great parent.

Big Problems? Find Hope!

The solution to adult problems tomorrow
depends on large measure upon
how our children grow up today.

Margaret Mead

Everyone I know has problems. Life is like that.

Seriously, there is not a person that I know rather well who does not have some kind of issue that stays with them daily and usually throughout their entire life. The problem may change, but we all seem to carry something in our lives that can make our heart heavy.

Those problems can be of many different kinds.

1. Drugs
2. Divorce
3. Death
4. Disease
5. Disabilities
6. Disasters

Some problems jump into our lives through no fault of our own. The wildfire that destroys our home and possessions is not within our control, but can create massive difficulties.

An addiction to alcohol can be our choice, and the problems that follow are the result of personal decisions either to indulge in momentary pleasure or fail to seek professional help.

In either case, it is likely that you or your children have something that must be dealt with on a daily basis. Life is not always easy, and the normal problems of being alive can make good parenting even harder to attain.

Decide to deal with it.

It almost sounds harsh, but when facing those seemingly impossible problems, we need to make the choice of confronting the ongoing problem in a way that the rest of our life is disrupted as little as possible.

Those choices are not always easy, but they are choices.

Our mind matters most, and the attitude we choose to adopt will affect the entirety of our life.

For instance, one of my friends lost an arm in a farm accident when he was a young child. Rather than bemoan his fate and stand on the sidelines of life, he chose to deal with his loss as simply a modification of some normal activities.

He became a pastor, built buildings, repaired cars, built grandfather clocks as a hobby and was an excellent pitcher and hitter on our softball team.

His problem was always there, but his mindset transcended sympathy and depression.

Defeat depression.

When your problem becomes your passion, the risk of depression sneaks into your life. Emotionally healthy people are not immune from problems. They deal with them in a way that either solves the problem or makes it bearable. Even if the problem continues to exist, they acknowledge it, but put it in such a perspective that the rest of their life continues in a reasonably normal and productive manner.

Strong emotional and mental courage enables you to confront a problem appropriately, yet not be consumed to the point of defeat. You do not have to pretend the problem does not exist; you simply have to keep it in a place where you continue to function properly in the rest of life.

That is not always easy, and you may find the need for some strong friendship support or even professional counseling, but it is possible.

Be patient, be strong. Overcome.

What does this have to do with grades?

Whether you are the one with significant problems, or your child is the one dealing with these things that can upset normal living, the approach you take to the problems has a significant effect on the level of success (or failure) in the normal activities of life, school included.

Perhaps your teenager did something really stupid and is in trouble with the law. Court cases are coming, perhaps even juvenile detention or problems you face for not controlling your child.

You and your child have a problem. A big one. And one that is going to change some things in your life.

Yet life still happens. There is a long way to go. There is even tomorrow to deal with.

You face serious decisions in how to deal with the situation, and those decisions are going to impact the actions and relationship between you and your child for the rest of life.

Are you going to defend those stupid teenage actions or give strong emotional and physical support as your child deals with the consequences?

The memories and realities of that problem will be continuing, but there are other areas of life that need to be completed successfully.

Preventive Parenting.

You are the parent, you kid is the child. That simple fact gives you the right, indeed, the obligation, to intervene in creating proper behavior and diminishing actions that you know to be detrimental.

Bill Cosby, the comedian, activist and now dealing with his own set of problems, summed it up nicely when he said, "Kids are like homeless people - no job, no responsibility, and no house."

They are living in your house, supported by your income, thus are your responsibility. And you have every right to raise them in the proper way.

Too much TV? Turn it off.

Video games all night? Confiscate the equipment.

Caught "sexting?" Goodbye smartphone.

Have you had "The Talk?"

Speaking of sexting and big problems, there is one stupid decision that inevitably has life-long ramifications.

Two teens, one boy one girl, at home alone or out on a secluded date... and the pregnancy happens.

Now what?

Chances are the guy disappears into the oblivion of wherever teenage boys go after becoming a baby daddy. The girl now has the big questions to face.

Is abortion an option, with the likely life-long guilt or wondering that will follow?

Should the child be put up for adoption?

What about raising the child as a single, teenage mother?

Even if the boy stays around, questions of marriage or living together, maybe even with Mom and Dad arise.

Obviously, a new set of problems that radically change lives are now on the scene.

This is one of those issues where "The Talk" becomes crucial. There is no magical right time to address this issue, but one principle is generally quite appropriate. When your child, even at a young age, asks a good leading question, NOW is the time to give an answer appropriate to their age level.

Chances are pretty good that as the child gets older the questions become more specific. Each time your response can expand into the reality of the wisdom of waiting for marriage for sexual relationships.

Chap. 5 - Students: The Present & Future Hope

Stephen Hawking

The writing on the bridge abutment said, "Come to my LIFE SUCKS party."

I passed it every day on my way to school. On a cold December morning I saw an addition to the invitation that said, "Tuesday - 4:20."

In the following days I kept building images of what that gathering of obviously disgruntled teens would be like. My mind held visions of pseudo-punk, pot smoking baggy-jeaned kids huddled in one of the semi-secluded parks near us.

The total disconnect between how cool they felt and the reality of how shallow and depressed their lives actually were was ominous and rather dark.

A bridge to nowhere.

Near Azusa, California, there is a bridge that goes nowhere.
Literally.
No road goes to it, nor does one leave on the other side. The bridge is a result of political boondoggling in which considerable effort and energy were exerted with no real destination in sight.
The bridge got built.
The purpose remains hidden.

Lots of energy and work resulted in a nowhere trip.

Real bridges go somewhere. They have a purpose. Real bridges take the traveler over a hazard and actually make progress towards a real destination.

Where does your bridge go?

In theory, your high school years are a bridge between the hormone-developing middle school time towards the maturity and reward of adulthood.

Crossing real bridges can be beautiful, providing a picturesque view of canyons and rivers while leading to new and exciting adventures. Some bridges are ancient and decaying, appearing unsafe for any kind of traffic. Those bridges may not be perfect, but they do get us to the other side.

What is the bridge of your life like right now?

Is it an exciting ride, leading to a better place?

Or do you feel like joining the "LIFE SUCKS" party?

If your life is going nowhere, it is time to fix it.

Get a grip on reality and join life in a way that has meaning, excitement and maybe even an adventure or two along the way.

Victim or Victor?

On an enjoyable day of swimming Joni Erickson dove into the Chesapeake Bay a vibrant, optimistic teenager. She emerged with a broken neck that left her paralyzed from the neck down.

Somehow, dealing with a lifetime of potentially depressing physical problems, she lives now in southern California with her husband, and has accomplished the following.

- written several books
- become an artist
- formed "Joni and Friends"

Her books have inspired people on every continent, and her service ministry continues to provide and distribute wheelchairs worldwide to those who cannot afford them.

Joni has crossed many bridges in her life, always leading somewhere.

Her journey has not been easy, but the destination has always remained crystal clear.

Lloyd Newton grew up minus most of one arm lost in a farm accident when he was three years old. Later, an automobile accident left him in almost continuous neck pain. Rather than complain about his bad luck or rely on others for help, he became an active pastor, played softball, built buildings and had a hobby of building Grandfather Clocks.

Those two people could have engulfed their lives in self-pity, yet understood that their apparent disabilities were simply "extra added attractions" to be dealt with on the way towards experiencing a productive, service-oriented life.

They approached life with a victorious attitude rather than indulging in a defeatist, "I am a victim" attitude.

Almost everyone I know has something really tough to deal with. Some of their demons are external, others rise from deep inside.

- Unfaithful boyfriends or girlfriends
- Cheating spouse
- Serious addictions
- Divorced parents
- Natural disasters
- Mental or emotional issues
- Learning difficulties
- Home foreclosures

The list could continue, but the point is that at some time, tough problems will intersect our lives.

Dealing with Difficulty

If they aren't there already, those tough times will come.

How you deal with them will determine the quality of your life. If you pull the "woe is me" approach, you will guarantee the norm of your life will become negative and depressing.

If you choose a victorious attitude, life can be fulfilling for yourself and beneficial to others... in spite of the circumstances you are facing.

Get a Grip. Join Life

Life can be hard, but it doesn't have to defeat you. The first step in becoming a victor rather than a victim is to understand that the Mind Matters Most. Your attitudes and actions are your choice. If something bad happens, it is YOUR mind that determines your response.

There are some fundamental, yet specific, things you can decide to do that will enable you to keep your mind focused on making good decisions.

- Understand it isn't all about you. Everyone faces something. And how we react determines the path towards victory or defeat.
    - ✔ Choose wisely.
    - ✔ Choose courageously.
- Determine to solve problems rather than let them defeat you.
- Divorce is one of those tragedies of life that affect many people. Before you marry, or right now if you are already married, determine that divorce is not going to be an option. Commit to solving problems rather than running away from them.
- Quit hanging out with Tina and Mary Jane. Seriously, doing drugs makes you dumber than a bong. Addictions are insidious, creeping into our lives quietly and appearing to bring pleasure. Deep in your mind, you know drugs are a nowhere trip, a bridge without benefit. Use your mind. Make smart decisions.
- Get outside help if you need it. Some problems have captured our mind and emotions to the point that we have lost the ability or will to escape. When that situations a friend, a pastor, a counselor can become a life-saving person. The hardest step in getting help is the first step.

Envision victory.

Each day you spend wallowing in self-pity or selfish indulgence digs a deeper pit of eventual disaster that gets tougher to climb out of.

Spend time building a vision of who you want to be three years from now... twenty years from now... what legacy do you want to leave.

Your mind really does matter most. What you envision in your moments of lucid thought is the first step in getting there.

It isn't automatic. It might not be easy.

But your life can become great!

Consume or Create?

Check out your purse or pocket.

- Smartphone?
- Snapchat calling?
- Thousands of songs?
- Texts waiting?
- Crazy videos>

Just think, a series of ambitious and creative people used their minds and talents to produce those devices that you use for a continuing cycle of enjoyment.

At your fingertips is an unending source of electronic information encompassing the spectrum of human indulgence or usefulness. And your only responsibility is to make sure the batteries are charged.

Creative and ambitious people invent and build these devices for many reasons.

- The potential for profit.
- The excitement of discovery and invention.
- Providing service to others.
- To fulfill the inner need to create.

Unfortunately, the Law of Unintended Consequences intervenes and these devices designed to be entertaining and effective have contributed to the dumbing down of our culture. For instance, rather than taking the time to read a good book, it has become more enjoyable to play inane smartphone games .

Even with unfathomable amounts of information at our fingertips available from the electronic universe, we seldom search deeper than the first page of Google, even if the information we see is not the best available.

Looking at the growing number of people who are ensnared by their

EED's (Electronic Enjoyment Devices), it doesn't take a rocket surgeon to see that we are creating an "Intellectual Caste System."

By that I mean a society where a decreasing percentage of creators are producing wonderful devices bringing a growing percentage of consumers into an enjoyable form of mind-dulled intellectual slavery.

So how about you?

Are you enslaved by electronic enjoyment?

Or can you actually quit texting and start talking?

Are you "best buds" in your ears, or do you have real-person friends with whom you can actually have a verbal conversation?

Let's be honest here... druggies live with an internal disaster if their next fix is going to be delayed for a day. How about you? What is your inner life like if you forget to bring your smartphone to school? Can you handle it?

There is a maximum mind-divide here. There are creative folks who think, act and produce. There are others who sit, react and consume.

Which side of the divide do you live on?

School Stuff

Many students think the "stuff" they are supposed to learn in school is unnecessary and useless. Teachers and parents attempt to counter that argument, even though it's the wrong argument to go against. Mathematics is one of the biggest issues creating the valid question about using it, and the response, "You never know when you may need math." is one of the lamest answers ever given.

"When am I ever going to use this?" is the whining question constantly being asked.

"Maybe never." is the honest answer. But it is the honest answer to the wrong question.

The better question is, "How does what I learn in school help me live a better life?"

Believe it or not, there are people who live a very nice life, but can't tell you the name of the tenth president or how to solve the quadratic equation. What they can do, however, is benefit from the positive habits they learned and developed in school.

- learning to listen intently
- maintaining their responsibility
- doing things on time
- discovering how to think critically
- doing uninteresting tasks well

The list could continue, but you get the idea.

Success trumps stuff.

The ultimate benefit of school is the level of success you achieve by learning how to do the right things at the right time in the right way.

Done properly, school can empower you with the following.

- Learning how to perform with excellence without the need for enjoyment.
- Discovering your best learning style.
- Knowing how to adjust to different leadership (teaching) styles.
- Developing character traits of persistence, patience, passion and integrity.
- Building a strong resume of references, academics and extracurricular activities.

You EARN the right to success.

Living in this age of entitlement we think society "owes us" a personal level of success simply because we are a living, breathing person.

The Declaration of Independence says, *"We hold these truths to be self-evident, that all men are created equal, that they are endowed by their Creator with certain unalienable Rights, that among these are Life, Liberty and the pursuit of Happiness—"* If you continue reading your see the nature of the Declaration turns more toward governmental interaction rather than focus on the individual.

Therefore, after the "...life, liberty and the PURSUIT of happiness..." we are pretty much on our own.

It is up to us to achieve or abdicate.

You will never reach your success potential if playing "Call of Duty" keeps you up till 3 AM or you indulge in whacky-weed weekends on a regular basis. If your phone bill shows twenty thousand text messages per month, you might begin to think there is some wasted time there.

Nuts and Bolts of A's and B's.

There are some practical actions you can take to help assure you achieving a strong academic performance... even if you don't have a genius gene.

- Procrastinate later.
- Work first, play guilt free.
- Find a smart spot to study or work. (personally, I like a donut shop)
- Don't go overboard. Set a timer.
- Choose friends who help, not hinder.

I have had the honor of interacting with more than seven thousand students in my teaching career, and each one brings something unique to the big picture of being alive. May I share some of their stories with you?

Kids I have known.

I share these brief journeys into the lives of some students, and a couple of autobiographical, to give a glimpse into some of the inner workings of various people.

Susan – 1970

Her tears traced glistening rivulets down sun-bronzed cheeks.
"Mr. H., I'm going to flunk physics." she sobbed.
"Susan, you're not flunking. Your average is almost 90." I tried to reassure her, surprised at the worry she appeared to have.
"You don't understand," she said almost in a whisper. "I'm choosing to flunk."
With that, amid sobs and tears, she explained how her friends had labeled her "snobby Susan" ever since the beginning of the semester when she had broken from the grasp of the general level classes to enter

the college prep classes. Susan desperately wanted out and back in the classes with her friends, but her parents, knowing her ability, wouldn't let her drop from the college prep class.

Her parents wouldn't let her drop. Her friends wouldn't let her forget.

Susan finished the year with an average of sixty and accomplished her goal of failing the class.

Blake – 1984

Blake was trying to explain to me the mini-war that had created numerous clashes in the halls of our small town, rural school.

"It's the jocks against the nerds, Mr. H." he explained patiently, trying to justify why he was being suspended for two days as a consequence for beating up a classmate. Trying to elicit my understanding and also convince me why he shouldn't be penalized for missing chemistry, Blake's words were precisely formulated and well-spoken.

At two-hundred-twenty pounds, just over six-feet, and an impressive athletic presence as leading tackler on the football team, Blake also had a solid A-plus average in Advanced Placement chemistry. As captain of the football team he felt an obligation to lead in this brewing battle, even if the path down which he led wasn't exactly where he wanted to go.

Even in his stress as he sought my sympathy, Blake couldn't resist a chuckle as I finally asked, "Tell me, Blake, are you a jock or a nerd?"

Autobiographical – 1953

It was my first day in the big school. Seventh grade. Mrs. Monroe's morning homeroom.

Having spent my first six grades with ten other students in the one-room school up in Bakers Mills, I was marveling at twenty-six kids being in the same grade, much less the same room.

"Hi, my name's Tommy." One of the kids who sat right in front of me said. "I'm from the village." he said, indicating the big town of over one-thousand people where the central school was located.

"Where you from?" he asked.

"Up in Bakers Mills." I replied, thankful for his friendliness.

"Oh, Dog Town!" His tone changed as he referred to the nickname our town had acquired from the time in history when dogs did outnumber the fifty-nine residents.

"You must be stupid." he sneered. "Ain't nobody smart from Dog Town."

Stan – 1974

"You gotta be S*%##@'n me!" Stan's eyes brightened as he watched the smooth stream of water from the faucet being deflected almost ninety degrees by the negatively charged rod.

Stan lived on a farm, milked cows before coming to school in the morning, and somehow ended up in my general physics class. Physics fascinated Stan. He even spent time in my room after school learning algebra so he could solve the physics problems.

Stan was a "closet intellectual," hiding from his friends his interest in academic things.

"Why don't you go to college, Stan? Study physics. Be an engineer." I probed one day.

"Mr. H., I'd love to, but I'm gonna take over the farm when Pop retires." he replied. "That's what I'm s'posed to do."

The next fall, when Stan was a senior, his father had a stroke. Stan quit school to take over the farm. Two years later the farm sold at auction. Stan went to work as a farm hand for his neighbor.

Today Stan is married to his second wife, has seven kids, and still works on the neighbor's farm.

Kevin – 1997

Kevin had been suspended from school for smoking marijuana and was still under suspicion for dealing dope. Now back in school, he sat in the front of the room on the left side table. He sat with his druggie friends. Slouched down in the seats and seething with anger, all three played the part perfectly.

Except for one thing.

Kevin often hung back after class. Waiting till everyone was out of the room, he would ask some question of science that had been mulling in his mind as he watched NOVA or Discovery Channel.

As the year continued an interesting syndrome surfaced.

Kevin would become intensely interested in a particular topic in class. He became quite vocal in class discussions, especially about general relativity and quantum physics. One day his body was leaning forward in total immersion in the topic. Suddenly, in a victorious moment of breaking away, Kevin picked up his books and moved to the empty table right in the middle front of the room.

Kevin still hangs with his buddies in the hall. But there's hope.

One More Autobiographical – 1984

I was attending my first chemistry teachers' conference since making the transition from twenty years in public school to a private Christian school.

I had been successful in public school, having taught physics and chemistry, AP courses, been president of the teachers' union, chairman of the science department, chaired several district-wide committees, and presented several seminars and workshops at state-wide conferences.

Lunch was being served and eight chemistry teachers were sitting at a round table, introducing ourselves by name and the school in which we taught.

"Hi, my name's John and I teach at Faith Christian School." I said with some degree of optimism.

Joseph, from a large public school nearby, sat directly opposite me. He leaned forward in his chair, eyes locked on mine, hands gripping the table and sneered, "Christian school teachers are the most incompetent, stupid and ignorant people I have ever met."

Unknown Students – 2006

I was leaving my room as first lunch began in the large public school where I recently taught.

A junior student was about forty feet away when he shouted to his friend walking up behind me.

"Hey, Dude, you seen Jason around? Don't he go here no more?" he inquired loudly.

"Din'ja here?" his friend shouted back. "He got hisself shot."

What identifies you?

Each of my students has their own story, their own identity. I have been fortunate to have known so many fine folk, learning something from almost all of them.

In this world of learning how to be successful in school and the rest of life, there are some important questions you should ask yourself.

- What do you envision your life to be like in three years?
- What steps are you taking today to be closer to that goal tomorrow?
- Do you want your own kids to become the kind of student you are today?

There you have it. School doesn't have to be fun like a video game or enjoyable like mountain biking. But it can be productive and functional, leading to a more successful and beneficial life for you and your friends.

Rebel or Revolutionary?

So you're a teenager?

Is that a problem? Or a possibility?

As a teenager, have you ever wanted to be a rebel? Tell everyone to "Stick it!" Chances are there's something inside you that looks at your part of the world and knows things should be different. You know things should be different, but you don't know how to make that difference.

If that's the case, this book might be for you. Not to teach you to be a rebel, but to show you how to become a revolutionary.

There's a big difference, you know.

Rebels are mostly just against stuff. Revolutionaries see that things are wrong, but more importantly, come to the world with a better way, a revolutionary way, of getting things done.

Watch it, though, for there's a danger in becoming a revolutionary. You might not fit in as much as before. If you become a true revolutionary, you will more likely stand out from your crowd. They might think you're a bit different, even rather radical.

Thinking for yourself is the most important step in becoming a true revolutionary. You can't remain a victim of easy enjoyment. You need to search for that spark of energy that leads you to become a person who makes a difference, who improves the part of the world in which you live.

This book will not tell you what to think. What it will do, however, is give you some hints and procedures to show you how to think.

You are here on Earth to do good things for other people, and live with a focus of purpose that gives your life meaning and fulfillment.

There's something else about this book. You won't be treated like an idiot. It is assumed that you have the desire and ability to become an independent, critical thinker. And once your thinking abilities are energized, you will become enthused to take solid action on those thoughts.

Here's how it works. I (that would be me, the author) will share some of my thoughts about learning and thinking that have been put together as I've taught physics and chemistry for several (okay, many) years. Some of those experiences involve farm kids, others from inner city and typical suburbia kids.

You may disagree with my thoughts, but guess what… that's totally okay. The only criterion is this; if you disagree you need to be able to crystallize your thoughts about why you disagree, and what you would do differently. If you can do that, you're on the wonderful road to becoming the revolutionary that lives in your heart.

One thing I won't do is bore you with inane questions of the yes, no and maybe type. Sometimes I will share my own thoughts or questions. Other times I will simply pose a question that should lead to some type of discussion, even if it doesn't lead to a definitive answer.

There is another important thing about this book. I'm not going to talk-down to you, nor am I going to try and use a simplistic vocabulary so that it will be easier to understand. I will present ideas and questions that are consistent with your abilities and possibilities. If, in my writing, I happen to use a word that might be out of your vocabulary range, I will resist the temptation to replace it with an easier word or phrase. Either figure out the meaning from the context in which it is used or grab your trusty dictionary, hard copy or online, and explore a new way of expressing yourself.

The writing in this book is not formal. I will write much as if we were talking with each other sitting in those comfortable chairs at Starbucks. Neither will I try and jam my ideas down your throat. I will simply propose a thought and give you the opportunity to mull it over in your mind. Then, when the mulling is done, you will hopefully reach some kind of meaningful conclusion or develop your own idea or question.

Finally, remember this; it's perfectly acceptable to ask the questions "why" or "why not?" But along with the right to ask those questions comes the responsibility to listen carefully to the answer, then engage in a logical and meaningful dialogue.

The Biggest Academic Lie

Joseph Goebbels , Hitler's minister of propoganda, once said, "…if you tell a lie often enough, people will soon begin to believe it."

Such is the case with the teaching of evolution. Current textbooks are now saying that evolution is no longer a theory but is accepted by scientists as fact. Well, the fact is, there are many scientists who do not accept evolution as fact. There's also a bigger issue. If evolution is true science, then it should fit the criteria of the Scientific Method.

You remember it, don't you? The thing you struggled so hard to learn in seventh grade. Just in case you forgot, here are the main ideas.

- Observations are made about an event in the universe.
- A reasonable hypothesis about the event is constructed.
- Experiments are designed and conducted to investigate the event.
- If the experiments confirm the hypothesis, a theory is developed.
- More experiments are designed and conducted to keep testing the theory.
- After various experiments confirm the theory, it might become a law or fact.

Interestingly, no one has ever actually observed evolution occurring. The problem with that is the fact that, if evolution isn't occurring now, when and why did it stop? Or is it over? Did all evolution happen at once, then stop at once?

Then there's the little matter of the experiments. Has anyone ever designed and conducted a successful experiment that even gives a hint that evolution is right? If so, where is it published?

In the context of intellectual honesty, the same is true of creation. We haven't observed it, tested it or even come up with a good theory of explaining it from a human viewpoint. Thus we're led to the conclusion that maybe it has to be a faith-thing. There's no problem with that, since the Bible talks openly about the need for faith. The problem comes in when evolutionists want to get all over the case of creationists who talk about faith, but fail to recognize the fact that evolution requires the same degree of faith as creation.

An interesting thing to do with evolutionists is to ask questions, then wait patiently while they attempt an answer – or just remain silent.

A couple of good questions are these.

*If evolution is true and depends on the "survival of the fittest,"
then what was there in the environment that would lead man to
begin to write poetry or compose music?*

*If evolution is true and species changed to create a stronger, more
viable organism, how was it possible for different sexes of the same
species to develop independently from one another?*

Finally, for some really interesting reading, do an Internet search on the concepts of Intelligent Design and Irreducible Complexity.

Steps Toward Becoming Revolutionary

There's a danger in what I'm about to say, so read and think carefully.

There really is life that's above and beyond sticking your device buds in your ears or developing digital dexterity as you battle the villains in the most recent video game.

Rather than spend time sneaking your smartphone out during class to text your buddy for the tenth time in the last hour, how about thinking seriously about some of the following statements? There isn't anything magic about the following list. The words are simply there to start your brain thinking along a new track.

- Ask questions you really want to know the answer to
- Ask questions that cause someone else to think
- Ask questions that cause you to think
- Look beyond the obvious
- Read
- Write
- Analyze
- Serve
- Search for radical excellence
- Learn to work first, then play guilt free
- Talk with adults… if you can find any willing to talk with a teen
- Remain "childlike"… see Einstein
- Resist being "dumbed down"
- Dare to decry mediocrity
- "Get a Life" with meaning
- Stand against "Approval by Acquiescence" (Solshynitsin)
- Don't learn the "not" (basketball & study habits)
- Turn off the "flat-screen" syndrome

Got Life?

Real life is somewhat like Einstein relativity. It all depends on how you look at it and who is doing the observing. Interestingly, this inherently incorrect concept leads some observers of life to reach the dangerous idea that it doesn't matter what you believe, just that you believe it with sincerity.

This is heavy stuff.

Let's get something straight here. There are some people who live lives that are far removed from the kind of person they really want to be. From a psychological perspective, these people become the kind of person they THINK other people want them to be.

If you are not dedicated to become who YOU really want yourself to be, you will gradually adopt the actions and attitudes that you believe your friends want you to be.

Developing this type of personality leads only to a life of confusion and eventually to despair.

You are the only one who can choose to EARN the right and purpose to live the kind of successful life you know is possible.

In life, your mind matters most.

In life, most self-inflicted negative circumstances happen when we don't think. Something happens, and we react without a shred of thinking. For instance, you are riding with a group of friends, and someone brings out a joint. The next thing you know, the police arrive and your parents are having chats with social services.

Similarly, you and your boyfriend or girlfriend are alone... and nine months later there is a crying baby in the arms of a girl who is wondering why the baby-daddy walked away without a hint of helping.

Poor decisions don't have to involve those that appear to be major or known to be life changing. Something as simple, though equally wrong, as cheating on one question on one test can radically change your life. For instance, one of my high school friends had been accepted to West Point. He wrote down one formula on a physics exam, got caught and his appointment to West Point was rescinded.

One thoughtless decision. One life altering event.

The critical facts of life.

There are many characteristics of being human that separate us in remarkable ways from other living things and give us a special place in the universe.

- we are born... we will die... and we know it.
- we can love... we can hate... and we choose which one.
- we can create... we can consume... and we enjoy both.
- we can serve... we can freeload... and we continue it.

Birds tweet, humans think.

Even if you tweet, text or tell your social media friends every moment of your day, there should be some degree of thinking that goes into the messages you send. On the other hand, you biggest problem of the day might be finding an outlet to recharge your smart phone.

There are bigger, more insightful questions that live within us.

(1) How did we get here?

Are we the products of random molecular interactions or the creation of a master designer?

(2) Why are we here?

Is the "pursuit of happiness" limited to self-indulgent enjoyment, or does "happiness" have a larger meaning we need to explore?

(3) Can one person make a difference?

In a global environment with billions of people, what does it matter?

(4) Does True Truth exist?

In a society where those who disagree with others are labeled "haters," how can effective and meaningful dialogue occur?

(5) Where are we going?

When we exhale for the last time, do we simply become a pile of chemicals or does that part of us called soul continue living?

Chap. 6 - We Are In This Together

"Don't let the noise of others' opinions drown out your own inner voice."
[Stanford University commencement speech, 2005]

—Steve Jobs

Introduction

Life isn't always easy.

Sometimes we feel trapped, even out of control.

Stuff happens, and is hard to deal with or even comprehend. When our life seems out of control or spiraling downwards, we have this internal feeling that we should be able to overcome, or at least cope with, the travail that troubles us.

Even though we think we should be able to beat our problems, we often have something that prevents us from learning how to live a better life.

If that is how you feel, you are not alone. Many people feel the same inner turmoil that might be consuming your life, but somehow they seem to be handling their problems differently and successfully.

There is no magic bullet to fix all our problems. There might not be a magic bullet, but there are fundamental principles that can enable us to put our difficulties in perspective and live a better life starting today.

Read on and discover these principles and how to bring them to reality in your life.

Define Yourself

*It takes courage to grow up
and become who you really are.*

e.e. cummings

You are not defined by what goes in, but what comes out.

Obviously, our thinking can be affected by the multitude of signals entering our minds through our senses. Most importantly, those stimuli and events that enter our being must be run through an inner filter which controls the person we become.

Like it or not, people perceive our worth and importance by what comes out of us, by the actions and attitudes we display. We may claim to have great intentions in any area of life, but what we do determines who we are. We may *want* to accomplish tasks in a timely fashion, but if we are consistently late on getting things done, others perceive us as irresponsible and unreliable.

We eventually become defined by those thoughts we allow to live in our minds. When those thoughts are good and beneficial, there is a high probability of becoming the person we have defined by our inner musings.

It is impossible to have total control over all the items that enter our mind. You just can't escape certain signals.

- Highway billboards
- Language of co-workers
- Unexpected expletives

Other signals we have more control over, but not necessarily total control.

- Television and print advertisement
- Movie previews
- Radio programs

At the other extreme are those things over which we have full control.

- Our reading
- Movies we attend

- Music we listen to
- Television programs we watch
- People we hang out with

In the realm of defining yourself, it is obvious that what goes into your mind has the potential to determine the type of person you become. It is totally up to you to decide what is positive or negative. Your internal filter needs to be highly alert to deciding which things stick and which ones get discarded.

There is one other component of the melding of external and internal stimuli and thoughts which determine the kind of person we become. Some people inadvertently become the kind of person they *think* other people think they are.

The conclusion of this thing about defining yourself is fairly simple. What other people think about you does have the potential to define who you are. Similarly, other external stimuli can affect your overall persona. Most importantly, the person you are on the outside should be decided by who you are on the inside, and that inner person is fully under your control.

Or at least it can be.

The first step in defining yourself is to understand you alone are in charge of who you are and who you become.

It isn't always easy to take charge of your inner self, but it is possible. It is possible, and you can acquire the courage and strength to live better from the inside out.

Control EED's

The real problem is not
whether machines think
but whether men do.

B.F. Skinner

We have become a flat-screen society. From birth to body-in-the-ground, flat screens abound. Actually, even before birth we are the star subject in a flat-screen sonogram.

The flat screens we encounter have several common characteristics.

- An abundance of exciting visual stimulation
- Usually an expected emotional reaction
- Immediate follow-up with a new visual stimulation
- Never stopping for pensive meditation

With the amazing technology and graphic manipulation available to the creators of these productions, the visual effects we have come to expect transcend what could only have been imagined ten years ago.

The movie *Star Wars* may have been the first blockbuster event in which special effects took top billing over plot and character development. Currently the effects that titillate our visual imagination take precedence over the subtle character traits and "imagination only" effects used so effectively in Alfred Hitchcock movies.

There are some positive results of what we see on the screens that pervade our lives.

- We can communicate with Skype worldwide giving a sensation of being there.
- YouTube can become a great educational tool.
- Google opens the possibility of 2,323,432 sites in 0.04 seconds.
- News and information can be disseminated globally in minutes.

That is the good news. The negative ramifications are ominously detrimental to us as individuals and as a society.

- Many people are becoming incapable of savoring the beauty of silence.
- Critical thinking is becoming a lost art.
- We are experiencing the demise of creativity.
- There is a growing expectation of easy and inexpensive enjoyment.
- An intellectual caste system is being created.

The challenge of learning to live from the inside out is to understand and implement the method of using your Electronic Enjoyment Devices for good rather than being victimized by the negative attributes they carry.

You need to think deeper than flat-screen emotions and ten-second sound bites.

Think about it! To a great extent we even elect the president of our country based on those ten-second TV sound-bites edited to convey radically different messages from their original intent.

My teaching career started in 1963. Since then I have observed a growing number of students who have adopted a lifestyle of comfortable mediocrity. In my opinion, I see a strong relationship between the growing abundance of cellphones, and other inexpensive, enjoyable devices and this syndrome of mediocrity.

We have created an intellectual caste society in which a very small number of creative smart people have invented devices that are inexpensive, enjoyable and easy to use. Our use of those "smart" devices is resulting in an increasingly dumbed-down society almost incapable of critical thinking and analytical skills.

There are tangible actions you can take that help prevent succumbing to being made dumber and less creative by constantly consuming entertainment rather than producing creative things.

First, try putting your EED's away for one week. If that isn't possible, put a time limit on how much you can use them each day. Then stick with it.

One more activity you can do to help your internal life come alive is an event I did in my classes thirty years ago. Unfortunately, many of my students today are literally unable to perform this activity.

I happened on this concept when I was about twelve years old, and television had first come to my small hometown deep in the Adirondack Mountains of New York State. My friends got TV before we did, which resulted in the immediate demise of our Saturday morning fishing adventures.

They stayed home and watched cartoons,. I continued fishing, but now alone.

In retrospect, it was a blessing awaiting discovery.

One rather cool and breezy day I sought out a protected and warmer place to eat my lunch. Climbing about eight feet up onto a large rock, I discovered the top had a mild depression and was covered with a few inches of soft moss.

What a perfect place to settle down out of the wind and enjoy lunch in comfort.

It turned out to be a longer lunch than intended, and for about an hour, fishing took a back seat to reclining in comfort, watching slow moving cumulus clouds and savoring a multitude of interesting thoughts.

Several years later, after I became a teacher and more or less adult, I turned that experience into a thinking event.

When my students entered the room on this particular day, I gave a simple set of instructions.

"Take your notebook, and come with me," were the initial instructions.

After walking outside and down to a gently flowing stream behind our school, I added the rest of the assignment.

"I am going to walk upstream with you, and once we are out of sight of civilization, one of you will stop and sit beside the stream. We will continue that way until we each have a location from which no one else is in view." I continued.

Then the most important essential of the lesson was given.

"You will be alone for one-half hour. During that time you are to Sit, Think and Write." That was the entire set of instructions.

Many questions emerged; "how long does it have to be?" "What do I write about?" "is this a graded assignment?" I answered them all with the statement, "Your assignment is to Sit, Think and Write." I then placed the students in their solo positions.

After the half-hour was complete, we gathered back together. When their papers were handed in, I was thrilled to see that almost everyone got it. Their writings went well beyond my initial expectations and were the results of minds operating in freewheeling and creative mode. Some made sketches, others wrote poetry and one wrote a short story from the perspective of a fish observing the student.

Here is the sad part. That assignment no longer works for many students. They are incapable (at least in their minds) of sitting quietly and simply thinking for even a few minutes, much less half an hour.

Here is your challenge. Whether you think you can do it or not, try it. Find your own "alone place." Once you find it, go there. Take paper and pen. Sit. Think. Write. And leave your device behind.

You may be wonderfully surprised at where a mind free from the noise and chaos of society takes you. Enjoy the trip. Come back refreshed.

Come back from that mental vacation energized and motivated to let your internal-self start the process of defining the type of person you know you are, and who you want to become.

Become Someone Special

I don't fit into any stereotypes.
And I like myself that way."

C. JoyBell

You were created to be someone special.

That word "created" might be a hot-button word for you, but it accounts for many of the attributes that differentiate humans from the lesser living things. There are only two realistic options.

- You are a product of random molecular chance.
- You were created by a Higher Order Being (God?)

The thrust of this book is not to undertake a debate over creation and evolution (especially spontaneous generation), but to build a case showing how you feel about your ultimate worth as a unique individual could be tied to the worldview you choose to adopt.

For instance, choosing to live by a random-chance basis for your life may produce some tough questions.

- If I am a molecular accident, why should I change?
- If I am a molecular accident, can I change?

On the other hand, if your foundation for being alive is based on the existence of a Higher Power, your hoping for a "better life" could be fueled and empowered by the confidence of a power outside ourselves. If a Higher Power exists, it is legitimate to ask different questions.

- Is there a real meaning to life?
- If so, how do I discover that meaning?

In a related life-struggle, one of the main tenets of the Alcoholics Anonymous program is understanding how a Higher Power enables the addicts to gain the inner strength to overcome their addictive tendencies.

Furthermore, only the existence of a Higher Power provides logical reason for dreams, vision and purpose.

In our youth-focused society, it is critically important to know that this quest for purpose and vision is not limited by age. I have taught degree-completion programs in a four-year university, one of which was a class studying to become certified elementary teachers. The average age of the students was almost fifty, the oldest of whom was sixty-two.

I overheard one of this lady's friends ask her, "Isn't it a bit late to be thinking about becoming a teacher?"

Her words lightened my heart.

"Tomorrow will be later." was her optimistic response.

That enthusiasm was rewarded by employment in an elementary school after she graduated.

There is something special about being alive. You are capable of dreams. You can achieve goals you set. Your vision can become reality.

An important step in overcoming apathy, even despair, is to grab hold of the concept that you really are a special person. You were created to grasp the meaning in life and to become someone whose life is fulfilled and useful.

Believe it. Act on it. Achieve it.

Pursue Radical Excellence

I am trying to do two things:
dare to be a radical and not a fool,
which is a matter of no small difficulty.

James A. Garfield

Unfortunately we live in a society in which people who habitually do things in an excellent manner are considered radical. Mediocrity has become such an acceptable way of living that anything transcending the norm is considered unusual, often even a bit weird.

In deciding to live a life outside culturally imposed boxes or within apathy-induced norms requires more than a little amount of courage. Honestly, in many places, you have to be brave enough to be "outside the norm" in actions, attitudes and activities.

The first step in this process of learning to live life from the inside out is to realize THE MIND MATTERS MOST.

Do you get it?

Everything you do, everything you think, is determined by your mind. Sometimes we fall victim to thinking our thoughts and decisions are the result of powers outside ourselves. There are times we must make very well-defined decisions based on external circumstances, but even in those, we are the ones who use our mind to make the appropriate decision.

Understanding that simple concept is critical to understanding the bigger picture of how to take control of your inner life so your external life will portray a person who lives an enjoyable, productive life.

When I talk about Radical Excellence, I mean doing things that are truly excellent, but doing those things by returning to the application of traditional values.

You see, it is simply a matter of doing the right thing at the right time and in the right way.

Those traditional values are living characteristics such as the following.

- Integrity
- Timeliness
- Patience
- Persistence
- Passion
- Honesty
- Sensitivity

There are certainly others, but those are good starting points.

If you have a difficult task to accomplish, but one requiring patience, do you CHOOSE to be patient. Or do you use a bail out excuse and say, "but I'm not a patient person?"

To some of us patience comes easier than others. You might not be that patient person, but you CAN use your mind to choose to demonstrate more patience than you really want to normally. Don't become a victim of what you consider your weakness to be. Use your mind to decide whether the task you are attempting absolutely needs you to slow down, take a deep breath, and do it with patience and carefulness.

Do you have trouble with that?

Maybe you should try practicing. Choose to do something that isn't too critical, but that requires some degree of patience. Try a fairly complicated puzzle. Put it in a safe place, then work on it each day until you get the entire thing done. Then you can step back, savor the success, and say, "I had the patience to complete it!"

Read the list of traditional values again. Decide which ones are your strengths. Commit to always living a life that continues to maximize those strengths. Next, identify any of the traditional values where you need to improve. Make an Action Plan to start working on that weakness.

Start small at first, keep working on it until success begins to be natural. As you try the process, soon you will savor success.

Develop Internal Confidence

Accept who you are; and revel in it.

Mitch Albom

In the Bible, Psalm 51 reads, "Create in me a clean heart and renew a right spirit within me…"

Whether you believe the Bible or not, those words ring true. We intuitively know when our internal spirit is free and clean. We also know when our controlling spirit is "right."

When our private thoughts and musings are positive and confident, it is much more likely we will become enthusiastic and productive externally. The fact is, we really do become the kind of person that our internal thoughts are producing.

If we abandon control of our lives to external stimuli, an insidious cycle begins.

We observe and experience the external world. Then we let our internal thoughts become controlled by that outside environment. Finally, as we think inside, our external self becomes defined by our thoughts inside.

You must always be asking, "Am I making the decisions about who I am based on my own logic and reason, or am I giving in to dwelling on external stimuli?"

If another driver cuts you off in traffic, how do you respond?

Do you shout out the f-word, give him half the peace sign and get all tense inside?

Or do you calmly pay attention to your own driving, thanking yourself that you have the serenity to not let a driving idiot raise your blood pressure or control your emotions?

The real key is this; you are the one who chooses either of those responses. The other guy didn't "make" you be angry or calm. It was your choice, nobody else but you.

Physical Events Affect Internal Response

There are some external things that you are in charge of that do have an effect on your internal being. Our physical well-being can affect our ability to respond properly to other external stimuli. You can start by paying attention to the following.

- Eat a healthy diet
- Perform adequate exercise
- Get enough sleep
- Keep mentally active

Life is not always simple, and there may be certain things that constantly drag you down or overwhelm your being.

- If too much TV is a problem, set a timer to establish a limit. When it rings, TV is off.
- You know you weigh too much? Start dieting today.
- Certain friends drag you down? It's easier said than done, but find new friends.
- Are you the proverbial couch potato? Don't just sit there. Do something. Anything.

Learn Psycho-cybernetics

Maxwell Maltz, a successful plastic surgeon in New York, found that even after a face lift, patients often felt bad about their appearance for psychological reasons. Maltz realized they were in need of a "psychological facelift" by improving their self-image.

In 1960 he wrote *Psycho-Cybernetics,* and introduced the analogy of the brain as a "servo-mechanism" guiding us to fulfill our self-image much as a computer guides a missile to its target.

Your self-image gives your brain direction and helps you create tangible goals to achieve the type of life you envision. A key component of using your mind properly is to build vibrant, positive images of what you want to become. If you are tense, stressed, or anxious, it will be more difficult to picture positive images. The more you relax and release tension, the easier you will picture your goal images.

A powerful method of visualizing your goals and bringing them to reality is to verbalize them to others, or at least write them down in great detail. Even spend time describing your goals to yourself. As you continue to envision with your inner self, it becomes much more likely that you will take the external actions needed to accomplish your goals.

Some people fear the creation of powerful visions. They even think by envisioning goals, they will become so focused on accomplishing their goals they will lose their freedom to live spontaneously.

That is a ridiculous thought. By developing positive visions and goals, we confront the reality of what our life has been. And by facing the truth of where we really are, we can deal with the contradictions that exist within us.

If you are having trouble creating positive vision for your life, it may be the friends you are hanging out with are simply dullards and wanna-be -cool kids. You don't necessarily need to drop all those friends, but it might be time to get to know some visionary kids.

To learn more about how powerful your mind can be in setting and reaching your goals, I highly recommend reading the book, *Psycho-Cybernetics.*

Find Freedom Inside

Sylvester Stallone

There are three definitive steps you can take to provide an internal freedom in your life. Internal freedom can then be the next step you need to experience in order to produce positive paths to production.

Pay it Forward

The concept of paying it forward is a great mechanism for allowing one good act to spread throughout many people, rather than just the one for whom the initial good deed was done.

Wikipedia quotes a letter from Ben Franklin explaining the concept nicely.

> *"The concept was rediscovered and described by Benjamin Franklin, in a letter to Benjamin Webb dated April 25, 1784:*
> *I do not pretend to give such a Sum; I only lend it to you. When you meet with another honest Man in similar Distress, you must pay me by lending this Sum to him; enjoining him to discharge the Debt by a like operation, when he shall be able, and shall meet with another opportunity. I hope it may thus go thro' many hands, before it meets with a Knave that will stop its Progress. This is a trick of mine for doing a deal of good with a little money."*
> *From: http://en.wikipedia.org/wiki/Pay_it_forward*

At a normal-person level, I remember my father starting a "pay it forward" chain when I was still a child. We were riding home from somewhere late one night along a dark Adirondack road when my father stopped and picked up a hitchhiker. Though we were poor, this man was even poorer and lived in a still-unfinished home about five miles up the road from us.

In normal conversation the hitchhiker casually mentioned he didn't have enough money to buy milk and bread for his kids. Without making any grand statements, my father reached into his pocket, took out his last five-dollar bill and handed it to the man.

"Here. Get some food from Roxy's store in the morning." were my father's only words.

The man objected, saying he couldn't pay it back until he got some work.

Never one to use many words, my father quietly said, "It's okay. Help somebody else out when you get work."

I knew we were having tough times financially, and my father never mentioned that to the guy, nor did he say anything to me. The message my father sent didn't need words of explanation. It was there for me to put deep into my soul.

Perform Random Acts of Kindness

Doing something unexpected and kind for someone you may not even know is an internally freeing act. Somehow, when you perform a kind act, your inner being takes a significant step towards a freedom than transcends explanation.

My daughter illustrated that concept one Sunday morning after church.

She, my son and his family and my wife and I would often meet at a restaurant for a late morning breakfast after attending church. One morning my daughter was quite late in appearing at the restaurant. After some reasonable delay, she walked into the restaurant with Charles in tow.

Charles was one of the homeless street people in our town. Marla, in a moment of God-prompted generosity, had stopped and invited Charles to share breakfast with us.

Once over the first semi-shock of our unexpected guest, our conversation was interesting and enlightening as we learned more about the real person, Charles.

Little Acts of Love

Recently, my wife and I cleaned out our attic. We dealt with the trauma of finally bringing ourselves to discard some of the boxed up mementos that had lived in our attic for many years.

Not everything got thrown away. My wife held onto a box of little notes I had written her while in college. Notes written, not for official reasons like birthdays and holidays, but simple words and drawings expressing my love for her.

As I watched the wonderfully nostalgic look on her face while reading them over, I felt pangs of guilt surge through my heart.

"Why did I ever stop sending those little acts of love?"

There was no viable answer for that unspoken question, and I made a quiet resolution to try and resurrect that habit. Not only do those unexpected gestures of reaffirming love bring joy to the person receiving them, but an internal freedom comes to the giver.

I can't explain the reason it happens, but perhaps it is the feeling that comes when you realize the one you love is receiving your message in a deep and meaningful way.

Whatever the reason, it works.

Why not give it a try?

Unleash Creativity

Great minds discuss ideas.
Average minds discuss events.
Small minds discuss people.

Eleanor Roosevelt

It is my belief each of us possesses creativity. Some just have the ability to release their creativity quickly and efficiently. Your perceived lack of creativity may be more a fear of making mistakes or being worried about public embarrassment.

There are things you can do to free your inner spirit and thus unleash your creativity.

Relax and Release

My nephew marks his golf balls with two R's, the tail of the second R ending with an arrow point. He uses that as a reminder to relax his mind and body during his swing. This relaxation allows him to release the club head through the ball and produce a long, straight shot.

The starting point for releasing your creativity could very well be addressing your need to relax your mind, body and emotions. Relax from the creativity-killing tension that holds your spirit hostage deep within your mind.

Change Your Place

A walk in the woods can do wonders for the spirit. Freeing the inner-you can be started by simply doing something different, perhaps even unusual.

If your routine has become a rut, you can climb to a higher plane by changing what you normally do. If you take a daily run or walk, do your route in reverse. Leave early and take a different route to work or school. If you play golf, tee off with a short iron and change the nature of each hole. Spend one day using your off-hand for things as simple as opening doors or eating.

You will be amazed at how simple changes in routine can lighten your mind and help you see the world from a different perspective. Seeing things differently is often the first step in letting your creativity become apparent.

Do Free-Form Writing

The minds of creative people do not live in little boxes. Constraining walls are broken down, and the inner person joins the outside society.

If you have a particular problem or project you need (or want) to explore, you can often start producing creative actions by sitting down with a pen and blank sheet of paper. Write the first thing that comes to your mind. Then the next. After that, the next.

Don't worry about structure, grammar or neatness. Draw diagrams, write phrases. Soon a pattern or structure will emerge.

Slow Down and Think

Life is frenetic. Everything moves fast. Finding a slow place seems almost impossible. Even our quieter moments are interrupted by text messages or obnoxious background music. Our minds have been hijacked by incessant noise, lessening our ability to think effectively and creatively.

You need to find your place, a place of quiet and solitude if possible. Find a place you can kick back and think. Turn your phone off. Take your "buds" out of your ears. Take time to think, to reflect and maybe even create.

Try Something… Anything

Creative people have full wastebaskets. That old phrase has constant truth. Another such phrase indicating the natural characteristic of the creative process is "the photograph that didn't end up on the darkroom floor." To update that concept we would now say, "the one that made it off the hard drive."

The point is simple. Creative people are not the least bit worried about making mistakes or are ambitious enough to keep trying things until the product they want emerges.

Even something like solving a math problem is relevant to this concept. If the problem is tough and you just sit there staring at a blank piece of paper, you are hindering any hope of finding a creative solution.

The key is to *do something*. If it isn't the right thing, it will soon become apparent. Then try something else. Keep doing different things until the problem is solved or the product is produced.

Let it go to get it back

Our subconscious mind is wonderfully active and efficient. Learn how to trust your mind to work on something while you are doing other things. Letting your inner mind go to work behind the scenes will often give you those serendipitous moments which thrill your soul and produce good stuff.

The key to getting your subconscious working, however, is to provide it with enough information to actually start working. That means taking the time to process the task or problem you want to address. You should make enough effort to bring your information close to what is needed to make productive work possible.

Then let it go. Relax. Get on with the rest of life. It might take hours, more likely a few days for the information to come back, but with the answer in tow.

The key to making this technique for releasing your creativity is to NOT PROCRASTINATE. If you wait until the last minute to start, most of the techniques for freeing your mind to be creative become useless.

If you are the kind of person who really is compelled to procrastinate, I have one word of advice… procrastinate later.

Some Academic Exercises

In order to get your creativity unleashed, you need to feel confident about the potential residing within. There are things you can do to reinforce your ability to believe you are fully capable of being a creative person. Following are three ideas just to prime your intellectual pump. If they aren't what you want to do, just get started by writing down three tasks you can perform.

- Write five titles for a book that could be written about your life.
- Write a poem or short newspaper article celebrating a task or goal you have already accomplished.
- Write a poem or short newspaper article celebrating a goal or task you have not yet accomplished.

Creative people have learned to never fear success. They also realize that failures are simply steps towards fulfilling their vision. The ultimate failure is giving up on your dreams. Temporary setbacks are just that... temporary. Maybe a mini-failure will give you time to slow down, think through the process, make necessary changes, then get on with the pursuit of vision and dreams.

Choose Courage

A ship is safe in harbor,
but that's not what ships are for.

William G.T. Shedd

There is a danger in freeing your inner being to the point that you are living a genuinely better life. Your inner freedom can remove tension previously limiting your ability to develop and share constructive ideas.

In other words, the previously hidden visionary ideas living within you will emerge for the rest of the world to see.

Your emerging visionary persona can become a threat to the *status quo*. Visionaries almost always upset those who are comfortable living with the "that's how we have always done it" syndrome.

When you risk presenting a new vision or even ask the question "why," you need to be prepared with courage to withstand the conflict that might arise. Even asking "why?" can be intimidating, especially to those who are addicted to apathy and content with mediocrity.

The positive part of that risk, however, is that you will be instrumental in accomplishing something powerful and beneficial to others.

When you generate visionary ideas, you may face the possibility of public derision, or at least being thought to be presumptuous at best or idiotic at worst. The worst part is the likelihood that some of those who ridicule your ideas may be colleagues, or even people close to you.

Only you know what ideas lurk beneath the surface of your external life, and only you can create the freedom of your inner self to allow those ideas to become reality.

You can perform a simple mental exercise to help continue the path to living a better life from the inside out.

Find a comfortable place where you can spend some time thinking, envisioning and writing. Maybe your favorite coffee shop, sitting there with the brew you like best, is the place to be. Sit and sip for a time, put aside all negative thoughts or potential problems. When the time is right, you will know. Now write your thoughts as you imagine the most ambitious vision you can imagine. Begin to envision what you can do to bring genuine help to others. As you imagine this vision, don't worry about logistics or methods. Just imagine what could be.

Once the vision is firmly implanted in your mind and written on paper, now spend some time identifying a series of steps that can become goals on the way to bringing your vision to fruition.

From that moment on choose the courage to travel the inner path to a life that works wonders for yourself and benefit to others.

What you envision may be something beyond your personal ability to solve. You might not be the person to actually accomplish the actions needed to fulfill the vision. Your role might be as simple as going to the proper person with a suggestion. Your responsibility might be to choose the courage to ask the sensitive question in a public meeting or social media.

Knowing the when, where and how of a situation requires wisdom, insight and courage. Don't be afraid to speak up in the right time and the right place.

Discover Freedom to Serve

Dr. Seuss

Being free as a person means several things, one of the most critical is that you don't have to be all things to all people. As long as you follow governmental laws, generally accepted norms and treat others respectfully, everything else gives you the freedom to be the person you really want to be.

The inner path you travel can and should be the one you choose to follow. Unfortunately, we often acquiesce to becoming the person we think others want us to be.

When who we try to be conflicts with who we want to be, inner turmoil grabs hold of our mind. Living a divided life never works. The results of such a dichotomy can lead to confusion, frustration and depression.

The most negative result of trying to live a life that really isn't you is to blame others for the conflict you experience. Remember, you are not a victim in this battle. You are the one who chose to let your perception of what others think determine how you do this living thing.

You may have chosen to let others define your life, and only you can take it back. That process of redefining your genuine self might not happen overnight, but you can start the journey to inner freedom today.

There is an oxymoron nature to the process of freeing your life to be totally who you want to be. There are multiple paths to creative freedom. One path is focused selfishness.

"It's all about me." becomes your mantra. Life choices are oriented towards personal enjoyment and pleasure. You do the things you want to do. The needs or desires of others become secondary, if they exist at all.

A more positive path is to willingly choose to put others first, or at least, treat them the way you would like to be treated. The beauty of this path is that you travel it by choice, not obligation.

Choosing to serve others does not negate doing activities that you enjoy or benefit from. Being a servant simply puts the totality of life in perspective. It brings a healthy balance to your existence. As you serve others you will see them pass along your actions to others or reciprocate in kind to you.

Our society today is not naturally oriented towards serving others. The "what's in it for me" syndrome is predominant and often creates discord. By changing that culture in your corner of the world others will benefit, and your own sense of internal well-being will increase.

By choosing to be of service to others, you will be illustrating the profound difference between being a rebel and living like a revolutionary. More often than not, rebels are simply against the *status quo*. They offer little in the scope of positive change. On the other hand, a true revolutionary may reject the way things are, but offers an optimistic alternative to what currently exists.

Becoming a revolutionary and choosing to break from your inner prison of external perception requires genuine courage. Revolutionaries choose the courage to not fit in, but stand out. By doing the right things at the right time, you will stand out from the crowd. You may not fit in nearly as much as previously, but the reward of being free inside will outweigh any negative feelings you may have about leaving a destructive lifestyle behind.

The movie *The Sound of Music*, starts with a series of songs sung by Julie Andrews. The words of these songs create a litany of positive thoughts that can transform the way a person feels about themselves. The general tenor (no pun intended) of the songs portrays a woman seeking adventure and freedom, yet somewhat constrained by inner fear and the thought that there is an expected way she should live her life. (i.e. enter the convent and become a nun) The strongest message comes when you listen to the first fifteen minutes of the movie, but a listing of some of the key phrases below can give you a good idea of how the songs parallel much of which we seek in living a better life.

"…my heart wants to sing, to laugh like a brook…"

"…my heart will be blessed with the sound of music, and I will sing once more."

"…how do you catch a cloud and pin it down?"

"…what will this day be like…I wonder."

"…what will my future be…I wonder."

"…I always long for adventure, to do the things I've never dared."

"…I must stop these doubts, all these worries."

"…I am seeking the courage I lack."

"…let them bring on all their problems, I'll do better than my best."

"…I have confidence they'll put me to the test, but I'll show them I have confidence in me."

"…I have confidence spring will come again."

As the movie progresses, Maria serves the VonTrapp family dutifully, yet unleashes her courageous creativity to make a better life for them all.

You can do what needs doing in your life. Face your problems square on. Think on good things. Have the courage to use your influence and skills.

This is a good time to begin. Tomorrow will be later.

So this is the time.

Start releasing your creativity today.

Live confidently tomorrow.

My Story - Sometimes Miracles Happen

In February of my freshman year in college I slept an entire weekend.

It didn't start out that way. Returning to my room after an afternoon lab, I was simply going to take a short nap before dinner. That's how it started, but didn't end until I woke up Monday morning too late to attend my morning classes.

In that interval of time I did take two "wake me up" showers and took the time to eat a package of chocolate pinwheel cookies and drink a quart of milk. After each shower, however, I chose to lay back down for another "short nap." Other than those lucid interludes, I was in deep, non-restful sleep.

In retrospect, that lost weekend was caused by a rather intense encounter with serious depression. The cause of that depression was rooted in a classic inferiority complex combined with an unhealthy focus on my physical appearance.

You get it, don't you? Being six feet tall, weighing one-hundred-thirty pounds, having a coffee-stained temporary front tooth cap and perpetually duct-taped glasses can do that to freshman student from the desolate Adirondack Mountains of New York State.

But freedom wasn't far off.

Knowing I was close to leaving sanity behind, I did the only thing that made sense at the time.

Dropping to my knees, I cried out to a God I didn't feel especially close to right then.

I don't remember what I said, just that life was closing in and there was nowhere to run or to hide.

There was a freeing clarity, however, as I stood to my feet. The voice I heard may have been inside my soul, but the message shouted courage into my being.

"Quit being so selfish. You are too important to Me to let others define who you are."

From that serendipitous encounter, I have enjoyed the courage to become the person I was born to be.

That weekend and the resultant moment started me on a lifetime of realizing that our mind matters most and that a Higher Power beyond our physical being exists. We are the ones who make all the decisions defining the person we become.

If we abdicate that concept, we become victims of the external. All the arrows point inward and we turn into a person defined by others, maybe into a being we don't even like, but feel powerless to overcome.

This short book isn't meant to be a prescription to happiness or success. It is simply a sharing of the path I have followed that has given me the freedom to become defined from the inside out.

While never perfect, always with resident flaws, my strengths and weaknesses are comfortable in my daily walk through this thing called life.

Having been addicted to inferiority and selfishness, I sometimes relapse. Even in those moments, somehow I have the acquired courage to dig deep within and once more live better from the inside out.

Part 3 - *America, We Can Do This.*

I started this book with the analogy of top-down fixes to education being like duct tape ineffectively used to fix rocker panels on an old car.

Interestingly, duct tape was one of several common items onboard Apollo 13 used to save the crew of the spacecraft. Plastic bags, cardboard, a hose normally attached to a spacesuit were combined with duct tape to modify the existing equipment, enabling carbon dioxide levels to return to safe levels and bring the crew home.

Most importantly, these fixes were developed by managers and engineers who actually worked on the development and implementation of the complex operating systems in the Apollo spacecraft. Neither higher level authorities nor outside consulting agents were the facilitators of the successful modifications. It was a grassroots operation designed and applied by people who actually worked in that environment.

Empowered Excellence can Fix Education

The most effective CEO's and upper-level managers know when to let go of their perceived power and allow the grassroots experts to design and implement programs and systems that can actually work.

Such a proactive release of authority would be remarkably unique in the education world, but guess what, such a radical cultural shift could be the fix we have been seeking for decades.

In Part 3 I am proposing two radical changes in the systemic nature of the educational environment, both of which will require courage to initiate and patience to embrace. Changing established systems is difficult. Difficult, but not impossible.

These system-changing principles are,

- Being willing to Redefine Professionalism
- Implement Lateral Leadership

Redefining Professionalism will focus primarily on the role and responsibilities of classroom teachers. Becoming classroom leaders rather than managers will take some time to grab hold of the idea, and chosen courage will be needed to actually implement that leadership.

Implementing Lateral Leadership involves district-wide and building-level administration letting go of selected tasks. This willful, even encouraged, transfer of decision-making will take wisdom and confidence.

Chap. 7 - Redefining Professionalism

Harry Blamires' book, *The Christian Mind*, was published in 1963 and addressed a mindset even more prevalent today, as peaceful protests turn into violent rioting and looting. Idealists who call for law and order and upholding constitutional rights are ridiculed, even as the rioters are applauded by those in charge of the city.

Similarly, in established institutions, idealists who propose a better way of doing something other than standard protocol are often ignored, even mocked.

In his book, Blamires wrote

"Idealists are the most tortured people in our midst. We get along very nicely with cranks and foreigners. We are tolerant of rogues and criminals. But idealists - those people who insist on logically relating principle to practice, end to means, purpose to process, goal to route - we have no time for them. Literally no time." (p. 19)

Tortured idealists we may be, but as teachers we are also enthused optimists. It is within that context that I start the final portion of this book by proposing a three-step process that will enable the achievement of radical excellence, which in turn, will produce a system of Higher Order Learning in our students.

Good things seldom happen by serendipity or by acquiescence. Those events that seem fortuitous or spontaneous usually occur because of intense planning and effective training. The system of Higher Order Learning I propose is more than theory based on philosophy. I will urge relating philosophy to mission and combining mission with action that leads our students to the place where functional idealism becomes an important and integral component in their lives.

Idealism without practical action is, at best, empty rhetoric. American revolutionaries changed the nature of battle and thus created a new country. Similar muskets were used by both the British and the Revolutionaries but with different strategies, thus producing a radically different form of government.

I shall approach the task of creating a revolutionary change in education in three primary steps.

1. Redefining Professionalism
2. Understanding Tom's of Maine and Mission
3. Creating Lateral Leadership through Radical Excellence

There is an inherent danger in reading what follows. Actually two dangers exist. The first is that the reader will give a cursory glance and then say, "So what? We already do that." If that's the case, please step back, take a focused look, and ask, "Do we really do that?"

The other danger is that the reader will recognize the importance of what's being proposed, and make a serious and energized effort to implement the concepts in a classroom or entire school. The danger in making creative change is that some people just aren't going to get it. They are the ones who create situations which make idealists as tortured as we are. For those of you in this category my word of encouragement is to learn to savor the risk as much as the reward, and then get on with creating a dynamic inertia that produces effective change.

Redefining Professionalism

When Dennis Rodman played basketball, body piercing and obscure antics included, he qualified as the consummate professional. Qualified, that is, by the secular definition of professionalism. He was good at what he did and got paid big bucks for his endeavors. Doesn't get simpler than that, does it?

The oldest profession aside, the historically classical professions would certainly have excluded Mr. Rodman and his potpourri of tantrums and tattoos. Doctors, lawyers and clergy were those careers afforded professional status as our divergent society began developing. At some point in time the teaching profession was at least nominally added to that austere list.

In the early days of teacher unionization the battle became divided along professional versus labor lines as the NEA and AFL-CIO clanged swords over who controlled various aspects of teacher power. The old-guard of teachers cringed to think that many younger teachers were willing to align themselves with truck drivers and coal miners in order to achieve better working conditions, more political influence and higher salaries.

That battle seems to have leveled out a bit, mainly since the NEA has become more union-like, yet still retains the more politically correct designation of an *association*.

A more insidious foe lurks, not quietly, but almost greedily waiting to destroy any remnants of true professionalism. That foe didn't always exist, and can be traced in its formation to the actual lessening of classical professionalism as the new-professionalism of status and power emerged from the clash of dueling unions. The onset of teacher unionism in the early 1960's followed by the ejection of God from the public schools in the same era correspond rather ominously with the precipitous decline of SAT scores and the emergence of Johnny and Judy who couldn't even read the studies which documented how poorly they were being educated.

Currently we live in the age of standardized tests, state and national STANDARDS, and other supposedly quantifiable instruments designed to quantify student achievement. *Teaching to the test* and covering one's exposed posterior (professionally speaking, of course) seem to be the emerging order of the day.

New teachers enter the profession highly motivated to teach Johnny to read, even if double digit numbers are still a bit vague. They enter highly motivated, but unfortunately, an unacceptably large number leave after minimal time in the profession, frustrated with a system that promotes the antithesis of good learning.

There is no panacea for this plight. We've dug an engulfing pit of societal confusion in which blame is passed, fingers pointed and responsibility abdicated.

Although there is no panacea, there might be a meager step taken in the proper direction if we regain, or perhaps acquire, a proper perspective on true professionalism. Then, if individual administrators and teachers act on this true professionalism, they will become better educators, and (surprise! surprise!) their students will actually become better learners. This won't happen quickly; not nearly as fast as society would like. If it takes twenty years, a full generation of teachers, we will have accomplished the task we choose to attack.

There are other factors that need addressing; parenting, student responsibility, school funding, societal mores, spiritual issues, even environmental issues. My intent in this book is to focus solely on the attitudes, philosophies and actions of individual teachers and administrators as we corporately acquire the proper perspective on professionalism. Once we understand true professionalism we will naturally get on with the production of Higher Order Learning in our students.

Looking closer at professionalism.

My orthopedic doctor friend defines a true professional as one who possesses a skill or has knowledge not possessed by the general population and is capable of being a purveyor of that crucial information or skill. The true professional has an intense desire and obligation to dispense this unique information or skill.

In September of 1963 I attended my first faculty meeting as a full-on teacher. Even as a rookie I was frustratingly perplexed as forty-five teachers debated for at least half an hour about whether to have chicken or steak at the fall teachers' picnic. Driving home that night I posed serious questions to myself about the nature of the profession I was entering.

A few years later, in another school, I listened equally perplexed as an administrator labeled one of the best teachers in the district as unprofessional. This administrator gave that harsh indictment because the teacher had worn hiking boots and jeans to school that day. Similar conversations became the norm, and being professional almost always involved easily identifiable characteristics such as clothing, handing in properly done reports on time, being on time to meetings and putting pictures on bulletin boards.

Rarely, if ever, did an administrator or teacher discuss professionalism within the context of enthusing and motivating students towards effective learning. Keeping classroom behavior acceptable and minimizing parental discontent seemed to be the benchmark of philosophical professionalism desired by most administrators.

Knowing there is something above and beyond hiking boots and being on time to meetings as the definition of professionalism has haunted me throughout my career. It's only recently that I've been able to verbalize the concepts that have been coalescing in my mind. I admit it's impossible to quantify the philosophical, yet I will take the creative liberty of categorizing what I believe are five levels of true professionalism in the world of teaching.

Level One: The Obedient Employee Professional

This person performs activities characteristic of an obedient employee.

- ➢ performs daily duties appropriately
- ➢ completes reports on time
- ➢ is on time to class and meetings
- ➢ keeps accurate classroom records
- ➢ teaches lessons directly from the syllabus or book
- ➢ asks questions from the end of the chapter

Level Two: The Creative Curricular Professional

The creative curricular professional

- ➢ conducts a classroom which enthuses and encourages student learning
- ➢ draws on the work and advice of others to prepare lessons
- ➢ modifies suggested questions appropriately for the class
- ➢ relates curricular material to daily living experiences

Level Three: The Activity Generating Professional

The activity generating professional

- ➢ dynamically integrates curricular activities into the learning process
- ➢ expands lessons and content into new and relevant activities
- ➢ is willing to risk trying a new activity
- ➢ imparts a sense of adventure into the learning process

Level Four: The Principle to Activity Professional

The principle-to activity professional

> ➢ starts with known curricular principles and produces new lessons
> ➢ modifies or changes lessons from year to year
> ➢ strongly integrates cross-curricular components
> ➢ enthuses students to risk trying creative learning experiences

Level Five: The Pioneer Professional

The pioneer professional

> ➢ generates new principles or revitalizes existing ones
> ➢ addresses the root aspects of HOPE learning
> ➢ applies new ideas to curricular content
> ➢ entwines curriculum with emotional and philosophical attributes of students

Like most categorically defined lists, no one person fits nicely into one section. There is always overlap and combining of where individuals fit into the list of blocks. Even as individual teachers have characteristics of each block, there is a strong possibility of a natural distribution encompassing one area more strongly than the others.

Obviously not many teachers will end up at level five. But all teachers should increase their professionalism beyond the first level. I will argue in the rest of this book that visionary leadership at the administrative level will create a system of radical excellence in classroom leadership that produces outstanding "Higher Order Learning" in students. This can be done by acknowledging and fostering the professional level acquiered by all employees of the school. This driving force of increasing professionalism should become the focused goal of the truly visionary leader.

Why We Teach the Way We Do

Once we understand the subtle nuances of an expanded paradigm of professionalism it becomes possible to verbalize the reasons we teach the way we do. It's critical that such be the case, for unless we can identify how our actions are related to our philosophy, that philosophy is simply shallow rhetoric.

A genuinely healthy school provides its students with an eclectic mix of teaching personalities and styles and its administrative leadership allows, even encourages, a vigorous mix of structure, freedom and innovation.

Though I've done this teaching thing for several years, I have not remained stagnant in either technique or knowledge about the process of learning. Face it, kids have changed. The flat-screen society is upon us, and while the special effects of Star Wars-type action are emotionally stimulating, the ability to think deeply and critically is fast deteriorating. Current and ongoing research in the arena of learning overwhelmingly supports that observation. For instance, Clement and Lochhead, in1980, in Cognitive Process Instruction, said, "We should be teaching students **how** *to think.* (emphasis mine) Instead, we are teaching them what to think."

Ironically, in 2001 the historical governmental push to have **no child left behind** placed an extreme emphasis on standardized testing. While not necessarily a bad thing, the factual content and mechanistic strategies in standardized tests do not address the viability of thinking deeply and critically while analyzing various topics and problems. Since the ability to think and analyze have a direct correlation between professional success and performance, it's incumbent on us as educators to give our students continuing and deepening exposure to opportunities that require deep and critical thinking.

We must never lessen the curricular content of our subject, but the equally important mandate for teaching is to seamlessly incorporate higher-order skills and processes into our classes. We must do that without trivializing or minimizing the curricular content of any given subject.

If you choose to teach in a way that transcends the norm there will undoubtedly be some people who simply don't get it. What seems to be relaxed and perhaps even fun, in their opinion, couldn't possibly be good teaching.

There's always someone who doesn't "get it," but be confident in your quest to teach from a Radical Excellence mode. The vast majority of your students and parents will understand and appreciate what you are trying to accomplish. For this you should be thankful and will be rewarded.

Transcendent Teaching as an Art Form

There is no magic bullet that enables our teaching to transcend normalcy. It takes seeking, learning and experimenting. A plane of teaching exists, however, that makes the effort totally worthwhile. A plane of teaching exists on which students acquire knowledge, learn to think deeply and, more importantly, walk away having an understanding that their worldview is the ultimate determiner of success.

That level of teaching exists when we envision our lessons more of an expression of an art form than a mechanistic regurgitation of curricular material. It doesn't matter what acronym we use or guru we follow. Once we comprehend the fact that our teaching must embody more fundamental principles than curricular content, then we are taking the first step in producing truly educated students.

Education ultimately looks at and analyzes the real world. Even in the abstractness of mathematics or the aesthetic of music, the real world entwines with our intellectual musings. From that starting point, I postulate that truly transcendent teaching arises from the finality of looking at life and the universe as an amazing opportunity in an infinite environment.

Having done the same thing and spent many hours thinking about the issue, I've reached this conclusion. There exists a level of abstract realism that, when attained, produces lessons that are truly outstanding. By abstract realism I mean a concept that isn't intuitively obvious, yet has a tangible reality that is integral to our true and continuing appreciation of the universe and our role in it.

I'm going to make a flagrantly inflammatory statement. For years we've rather glibly said that we focus on our students' needs and strive to produce people who are richer and stronger than they would have been without that intervention. Perhaps we've not seen the bigger picture, the picture that should hang visibly on the wall of public inspection, placed there for critical acclaim and enjoyment of those who pass by.

Now here's the inflammatory statement. The student should not be the focus point of our teaching. I've begun to think that the true fruition of essential teaching comes when we present transcendent lessons in astronomy, mathematics, literature, maybe even in the excitement that a biology teacher shows about turtle droppings! Lessons transcendent in subject-matter but reflective of real life is the vehicle for modeling enthusiasm, passion and relevance.

Do you get it? The student might be the goal, but not the focus. The lesson is our aiming point. When that happens, when our individual lessons, our classroom presence, our enthusiasm all merge into the natural teaching and illustrating HOPE. (**H**igher **O**rder **P**rinciples of **E**ducation) That's when the students get it!

Just as we savor the visual excitement created by black and white images of stark and barren mountains captured by Ansel Adams or bask in the music of Johnny Cash, Bach or U2, our students should have the opportunity to inspect our own classroom artistic endeavors. Done properly, our artistry performed with the brush of classroom presence can genuinely reflect and reveal the worth of a genuine life of service and reward.

It's a difficult task to teach students responsibility while simultaneously helping them understand the quantum nature of the atom. Sometimes it's a real battle to enthuse students with enough excitement to create excellence as they write papers or produce science fair projects. Preparing self-indulgent teens to perform well on the semi-sacred SAT's is a daunting responsibility. Yet to think that my lessons should transcend those mechanistic outcomes almost overwhelms me.

As I see it, there are a series of starting points, some philosophical ideas and practical principles will create an environment in which such artistry becomes possible.

First, each faculty member and administrator must see themselves as a member of the team, the body. We are here at this time and in this place for this purpose. Each one brings something to the group that makes us all stronger. Second, consistent individual motivation towards improvement will never return empty. Our minds and hearts will become knowledgeable and confident in the principles and concepts that, when applied, produce Higher Order thinking and acting. Next, continued search for the wisdom and courage to teach transcendently will always work as we move in the direction of understanding that teaching really is an art form.

If those are the philosophical principles there are also some nuts-and-bolts concepts that enable us to bring our students into a better and higher place.

1. Relationships enable reception. Put simply, students and colleagues listen and respond actively when our relationships are positive and trusting.
2. Classroom *leadership* is bigger and better than classroom management.
3. Curricular Comfort Creates Confidence. Wow! How's that for alliteration?
4. Serendipity follows imagination. As we expect positive things fueled by a creative imagination, events jump excitedly into beautiful teaching opportunities.
5. We must really know and commit to our mission.
6. We must savor the risk of teaching transcendently in order to anticipate the reward.

To enjoy the art of Monet, the music of Bach, the poetry of Sandburg requires an environment which allows the viewer to savor the moment, to inhale the beauty. The same is true in the classroom. All those pre-artistry events, the discipline, the content, the mechanics, they're like the steps leading to the art display. They are the processes which make the final appreciation of a transcendent lesson possible.

Such is the role of classroom mechanics. They exist to create an environment in which our students have the opportunity to learn of a successful life through the canvass of a math teacher's art, to experience the music as a history teacher expounds with passion about civil rights or World War II.

The naturalist John Muir wasn't a perfect person and a lousy husband, yet his immersion into the beauty of the natural wilderness radically affected his actions. That immersion affected his actions to the extent that the world is different as a result of his passion.

What a thought to ponder... that our passion to create artistic effort in our classes might someday cause a student to see the true potential in a life well-lived.

Chap. 8 - Implementing Lateral Leadership

The Road to Radical Excellence

*The quality of a person's life is in direct proportion
to the commitment to excellence
regardless of their chosen endeavor.*

Vince Lombardi

You may dislike the personality of Elon Musk, or even his style of aggressive leadership. The fact is, however, his leadership, almost single-handedly, grew both Tesla automobiles and SpaceX rockets into an international powerhouse.

The leadership of both Steve Jobs and Bill Gates created products which have influenced the nature of culture in an unforeseen fashion.

The point is simple; leadership is the most important factor in producing outstanding success. It is also, if done poorly, the most ominous factor in fostering the negativism of failure

The remaining sections of this book will address the main points necessary to produce a school that is committed to a system of Radical Excellence. From that commitment to excellence will come Higher Order Learning. I will explain and propose the following.

> ➢ Understanding Mission and Commitment
> ➢ The Critical Nature of Leadership
> ➢ The Concept of Lateral Leadership
> ➢ Implementing Lateral Leadership

Understanding Mission and Commitment

Tom Chappell was founder and CEO of "Tom's of Maine," a body and health care company which focuses not only on making a profit, but being environmentally sound and paying attention to the welfare of both its employees and the town in which it is located. The company is fully committed to its well-thought-out mission statement. In his book, Managing Upside Down, Chappell expounds on the thesis that **all** decisions of the company must be consistent with the stated mission of the company. He further defines the concept of "managing upside down" as "letting your own deepest beliefs and values... drive your business." Chappell goes on to say how every level of operation in the company, from the janitorial staff to the executive board, must make decisions that remain true to the mission statement.

Realizing that most companies and institutions have well-intentioned mission statements but that those good intentions often are ignored when day-by-day decisions intervene, Chappell has instituted a system which forms the basis for an ongoing training program for each and every Tom's of Maine employee. The "Seven Intentions" method provides values-based tools that enhance employee skills and performance.

"CONNECT WITH GOODNESS: Set aside your own ego, open up, and connect to a universal force that is bigger than you and available to everyone—the power of goodness.

KNOW THYSELF, BE THYSELF: Explore who you are, your gifts, and what you care about most in life. These are the clues to finding meaning in your work.

ENVISION YOUR DESTINY: Envision your future with your head and your heart. The Upside Down approach is to allow your business goals to emerge from who you are as a company, your essence, your reason for being.

SEEK COUNSEL: Tom's of Maine listens to everyone—its board of directors, employees, consultants, suppliers, retailers, and customers.

VENTURE OUT: Build a creative strategy for every dimension of
your new business, make sure it is aligned with your values, and
go for it— even if there is nothing like it in the world.

ASSESS: No matter how creative you might be or how unique you
are in the marketplace, you are still accountable to your values,
vision, and goals. Managing Upside Down is a trial-and-error
process, and assessment requires constant affirmation and
editing.

PASS IT ON: When you receive gifts, knowledge, goodness, extra
time, and profits, you are obliged to pass them along to others.
Along the way, you set up an exchange of experiences and a trial-
and-error process that can help everyone improve."

HTTP://www.tomsofmaine.com/about/values.asp

Wouldn't it be refreshing if schools held to the same degree of commitment to what they say their mission is? If what we *say* we do is so important, let's do it. Find a way. Put energy towards achieving the goal. Make a commitment to be committed to that wonderfully phrased mission statement, no matter what.

All I can say is this. Good for Tom's of Maine!

Backpacking and Schools?

Backpackers and hikers understand commitment. Breaking camp in the pre-dawn hours, slinging your pack onto your back, checking maps and water supplies you prepare to leave, knowing that to accomplish the day's mission will require overcoming fatigue, enduring great thirst and challenging extreme terrain. Your heart races with anticipation, not just for the view from the top, but for the journey. The journey is part of the reward, and there's an energizing confidence in knowing you won't quit.

Such is life on the trail.

Unfortunately such commitment is often not the case in many schools. Boards of education and administrators spend considerable time formalizing altruistic and seemingly sound mission statements. Written in the first few pages of school handbooks, those statements are there for all to read. Read, but often ignored during daily operation of the school. The mission statement holds the same status as a topographic map on which a route might have been drawn then placed at the bottom of a desk drawer, never to be taken on the trip.

In many schools commitment to mission is directly related to acquisition of dollars. As dollars decline so does attention to the task.

Quality costs. One of my public school colleagues holds to the theory that much of the problem with public school is that it's free. Or at least seemingly free to those who never actually hand over a check for the services provided. He maintains that "free" tacitly implies "no value," thus students receive the subtle message that their efforts are also of little worth since their perceived reward is minimal.

Quality does cost. And dollars are difficult.

A hiker's energy is high in the morning, and the pace is brisk. Afternoon always comes. The trail gets steeper. The energy drains. But the mission remains. Make it to the top. You stop for a rest, a drink, take time to savor the stress and the sweat. Then get it on again. One step at a time. Your back hurts, your legs quiver. One step at a time with commitment. You make it! The view is incredible, the accomplishment is indescribable.

When the trail steepens, you find a way.

The Critical Nature of Leadership

The second public school principal I had was intensely influential in many of the characteristics I took into my teaching career. When I was a third-year teacher he took me aside one day and we discussed the concept of being a leader in the classroom. His comments were clear and insightful.

"Don't ever forget, young man, that when you stand in front of your class, you are their leader. Way more important than a giver of knowledge, you are their model. Do it right and they will remember you for the rest of their lives. Do it right and you will affect their lives." were his words.

When our son left the classroom to become an administrator and then executive director of a therapeutic academic and wilderness program for troubled teens, he said one of his most difficult tasks was maintaining effective contact with the faculty and counselors. He has successfully overcome that hurdle by always focusing on the concept that the person who works directly with the students is in a leadership position, in the position to directly affect the lives of students. His leadership role is to facilitate theirs' and to infuse the classroom and field leaders with vision and energy, thus enabling students to be better served.

It takes a strong and confident leader to genuinely empower those who are listed under his authority on the boxed-in organizational chart. When empowerment happens, a solid relationship of trust and confidence exists, and the system develops an energy-creating excitement and effectiveness.

Unfortunately, many school administrators or principals hold to an archaic, authoritarian philosophy of leadership that stifles creative and courageous leadership in the classroom.

I wasn't there in the beginning of the public school movement, but I suspect the fledgling school had very few career teachers involved. The lack of potential classroom leaders mandated the principal and administrator become the all-knowing leader. Perhaps the only professional educator in the school, the principal, by necessity, had to become all things to all people.

Those days are gone forever. They're gone in reality, but I fear not in the perception of many current administrators. In the area of teacher evaluation and professional growth, there is still a residual philosophy that the principal or administrator is the consummate answer person.

Leadership is serious business.

As a classroom teacher I've had my own private chuckle moments as I've read evaluations of my lessons by well-meaning administrators who must have thought their job wasn't complete unless they offered some modicum of "improvement" suggestions.

"Good lesson, John, but don't you think it would be better if you had more than one eraser on the chalkboard tray?" was one principal's most severe criticism.

Another evaluating principal said, "I really enjoyed your lesson, but I did notice that the window shades in your room were not all evenly spaced. Since your room faces the street we need to give an organized appearance." were his words of advice. When I explained that the shades had been purposely placed that way to illustrate a half-life decay curve for radioactive elements and was part of an upcoming quiz, he said, "Couldn't you do that just as effectively by a paper handout?" missing the intended point entirely.

Those assessments resulted in mental, chuckle-filled reactions, but another one saddened me in its potentially disastrous consequences and lack of insight into the full meaning of teaching critical thinking from a worldview perspective.

My physics class had just completed a unit on Einsteinian Relativity and the development of the quantum nature of the atom. I had previously administered a traditional exam testing the curricular facts, concepts and mathematical analysis needed for that level of learning. The next day I gave an essay question as follows.

> *Based on your knowledge of the theory of relativity, the Heisenberg Uncertainty Principle, Bohr's assumptions about atomic structure, Plank's hypothesis concerning the quantum nature of energy and DeBroglie's hypothesis about the dual nature of matter and energy, explain why it is logical and understandable that a scientist could choose a relativistic and random worldview about the nature of life and the universe. Then explain a reasonable argument that could serve as the falsification requirement in their theories.*

Most of the students did quite well on answering the question and several produced truly profound answers.

When my principal inspected the exam he said, "That's the worst test I have ever seen."

He then followed with, "I think you should ask more questions from the end of the chapter."

Authoritarianism, tradition and mediocrity are safe attributes by which to live as a leader. Courage and risk-taking are not necessary when a comfortable *status quo* represents the highest plane of learning desired. Strong visionary leadership doesn't need to exist in the educational environment if first-level professionalism is the norm, maybe even the goal.

Ironically, many administrators who prefer a safe-system sort of school also tend to be reclusive and unwilling to mingle freely with the faculty. I've developed a quantifying method to identify the "hiding power" of such reclusive administrators. It appears rather consistent that administrators can be categorized by the number of doors between themselves and the rest of the school population. An open door type administrator is quite available, and usually a very confident and visionary leader. As confidence and courage decrease, the empirical and anecdotal evidence from my very limited observations indicates that the number of doors between the administrator and the faculty also increases.

Almost beyond belief, the most non-communicative, reclusive and authoritarian administrator I have worked for was a five-door man, and one of the doors was often locked! Furthermore, when we entered the five-door pathway to his office, it was often dark, the shades pulled and he was working somewhere else so he wouldn't be disturbed.

Hope Amidst the Absurd

There is hope in this world of absurd decisions and practices.
Thankfully, there are administrators and principals who know life in school doesn't have to be like that. There are administrators who exude vision, who empower their faculty and who adopt a communicative style of management. If you are that type of administrator you likely incorporate many of the techniques and practices that I shall propose in the rest of this book into your school. If you've only dreamed of trying something beyond the norm, the final chapters will present the outline of a model of management/leadership that I call Lateral Leadership. Most importantly, this model of operation provides an opportunity to produce Higher Order Learning in your students.

Where potential lives, progress emerges

Had he stuck with it, a high school principal I had from 1994 to 2004 would have become an outstanding administrator. A few years before he left high school to become a college administrator and professor, he wrote the following sentence in a letter to the faculty.
"My vocational frustration is having a collegial atmosphere but not the forum for more formal collegial decision making." were his

insightful, even if lamenting, words.

But he got it. He understood the concept, even though the lack of a vehicle for implementing those ideal philosophies didn't exist in that school. Compounding the frustration he (and many of the faculty) felt was the fact that a genuine spirit of collegiality did exist in the school. Other circumstances existing at the highest level of administration were present, however, that prevented moving in a direction designed to capitalize on that interpersonal relationship present in the school.

I am suggesting a model that, if implemented, can produce a school that draws on the inherent power of genuine collegiality, places professionalism in the proper perspective, and creates leaders at all levels of operation. Saying it one more time, the concept of Lateral Leadership can create Higher Order Learning in our students if it is actively pursued and energetically sought after.

Funnels constrict flow.

The historical model of school administration and operation is hierarchical in nature. Essentially all decisions of importance are funneled through one or more administrative positions. This is not necessarily bad, yet is predicated on the assumption that the particular administrator is the primary expert in almost all areas of critical decisions. Even when dialog between administration and faculty does occur, the compelling decisions are often made when the administrative group draws aside and determines the final outcome. This reclusive and authoritarian system does not produce the ownership necessary for the effective team-like nature of an energetic and effective school. While a perceived sense of collegiality may exist, the fact remains that it is in perception only.

The foundational weakness of the historical model is that the administrator, at whatever level, is placed in a position of having to be the resident expert in each of the different areas of operation. In the complex society in which we live and do school, the scriptural mandate to seek the counsel of many and to acquire wisdom from that interaction becomes even more critical, but is often totally ignored.

The Structure of Lateral Leadership

The basic goal of a Lateral Leadership System is to maximize the professional expertise of the staff of a school in the areas in which they are most intimately involved. Classroom teachers and every other employee of the school therefore, play an integral role in the development and decision making of school-wide instructional processes.

The framework of the Lateral Leadership System consists of creating seven Core Groups as follows.

- ➢ Professional Development and Evaluation
- ➢ Curriculum and Instruction
- ➢ Classroom Leadership and Management
- ➢ Student Growth and Discipline
- ➢ Social Life and Curriculum Integration
- ➢ Facility Management
- ➢ Public Relations and Parental Involvement

Each of these Core Groups will be chaired by one of the traditional Department Chairs or a faculty or staff person with particular expertise in an appropriate area.

Inherent in all levels of operation must be the alignment of the school mission statement with decisions or suggestions produced. If it doesn't line up with the mission statement, it doesn't happen.

Core Groups will have **immediate decision making authority** within the context of state and local legal statements. The primary responsibility of the Core Groups is to assist and encourage each employee to continue growing professionally and in expertise of their particular area of service. Open dialogue and creative growth tasks are encouraged and supported.

Part 4 - *America, We MUST Do This.*

After the Apollo 13 incident several internal changes were instituted within the technical and operational modes of the Apollo program. Those changes were important in future flights, but the total program had some politically and financially induced problems which brought it to an end.

Author Colin Burgess wrote, "the life-or-death flight of Apollo 13 dramatically evinced the colossal risks inherent in manned spaceflight. Then, with the crew safely back on Earth, public apathy set in once again."

Recurring almost in rhythm with political cycles, the problems inherent in the education world are placed on temporary life support systems replete with new acronyms and the inevitable increased cost. Unlike the Apollo 13 fixes, these duct tape and shiny new programs do not work and only add to the increasing frustration to the idealists among us.

Most alarming, however, is the recurring apathy by almost all stakeholders, stifling effective and lasting change in the inherent nature of education.

We must know and focus on the *Real Goal* of education.

The active goal of people at NASA was to get three astronauts back to earth safely.

It seems to me there should be one focused goal of education.

> ***We need to give students the opportunity***
> ***to create a life rewarding for themselves***
> ***and of service to others.***

If we are serious about such a noble platitude, we must reinstate a missing component which enabled historical education to be far more effective in achieving that goal than it is today.

Chap. 9 - Passionate Anticipation is Revolutionary

*"Do not let the memories of your past
limit the potential of your future.
There are no limits to what you can achieve
on your journey through life, except in your mind."*

—Roy T. Bennett, The Light in the Heart

Wayne Gretzky is one of the greatest hockey players ever. Asked what made him great, he said, "I skate to where the puck is going to be, not where it has been."

People have said of Steve Jobs his success with Apple was his ability to anticipate future trends.

Elon Musk saw a future in electric cars and inexpensive space flight and revolutionized both arenas.

False-Fix or Create; that is the question.

Education "reform" almost always focuses on fixing or slightly modifying that which already exists, but is now broken. If math grades are down on standardized tests, try a new math program… or at least a new acronym.

We desperately need a revolutionary change to the fundamental nature of education. Only then will what we do in schools have a profound effect on our general culture.

One at a time.

The Starfish Story is a mini-classic in motivational culture. I repeat it here as told on the website https://www.thestarfishchange.org/starfish-tale.

IT ALL STARTED WHEN...

A young girl was walking along a beach upon which thousands of starfish had been washed up during a terrible storm. When she came to each starfish, she would pick it up, and throw it back into the ocean. People watched her with amusement.

She had been doing this for some time when a man approached her and said, "Little girl, why are you doing this? Look at this beach! You can't save all these starfish. You can't begin to make a difference!"

The girl seemed crushed, suddenly deflated. But after a few moments, she bent down, picked up another starfish, and hurled it as far as she could into the ocean. Then she looked up at the man and replied,

"Well, I made a difference for that one!"

The old man looked at the girl inquisitively and thought about what she had done and said. Inspired, he joined the little girl in throwing starfish back into the sea. Soon others joined, and all the starfish were saved.

Standardized Tests and Herd Mentality

Individual schools receive data about the standardized tests their students have taken. Inevitably those results are categorically grouped by race, economic status and educational level. The natural result of analyzing such data is for an action-group to find ways to improve scores of one or more of the "disadvantaged" groups.

Talks happen, ideas fermented and well-intentioned goals presented.

Mechanisms for solving the problem often represent the same group-think syndrome; "we need more money, if only the parents spoke English and drugs are killing that community."

Then, in too many instances, teachers go back to the normal task of presenting curricular material to classes of forty-plus students composed of all the focused groups… and life continues as it was.

Ground Zero for a Cultural Revolution in Education

Almost every teacher I know can share multiple stories of individual students returning years later with encouraging words.

- "Thank you so much for the day you talked to me about dealing with my autistic brother."
- "I never could have become a doctor if you hadn't encouraged me to turn my dreams into reality."
- "You were the first teacher I had who dared to be different. It gave me courage to be who I really am."

Do you see the simple fact? Each former student who comes with those stories was a member of a group. Part of a group, **yet they acted as an individual!**

In every story like that the teacher did or said something beyond the curriculum, something which crystlized a character trait within an individual which initiated a journey to a rewarding life.

Those positive responses seldom arise because of the teacher's knowledge of calculus or the ability to understand paragraph structure. Real life-changing actions happened when some aspect of the deep character issues of life resonated with the need of an individual student.

Accident, Epiphany or Intent?

Positive ancillary events can occur in our teaching by accidental things of which we take adantage. Other times a spontaneous epiphany can lead us into an excellently creative lesson. And some days what we actually planned is carried off in an inspirational moment.

I propose, deep from my heart, a radical, truly revolutionary concept in the world of teacher training and professional development.

*We need to develop and implement strategies and actions showing students **their mind matters most** in developing positive character traits, giving them **HOPE** for a rewarding and service-oriented life.*

My parents, teachers and professors shared a common trait; they each chose the courage to talk openly and honestly about some of the big-issues of life. Thus it was natural and normal for me to do the same, even in my classroom.

When a student asked a question, it was only logical to answer that question with the same honesty and courage I had observed growing up.

As a rookie teacher, I quickly observed a disturbing lack of interest and curiosity in my students about the nature of life as it related to the curricular content being studied. To help generate some degree of thinking more deeply about the nature of being alive, I implemented a system of a one or two minute "thinking moment" discourse to start class. Doing this once or twice a week was effective in giving some students the impetus to ask insightful questions.

At the end of a class discussing the theory of relativity, one student asked, "If everything is relative, why do my parents and I have big arguments about smoking pot? It might be wrong for them, but right for me. Who cares what my life is like as long as it doesn't hurt someone else?"

The bell was about to ring, causing us to act like Pavlovian life forms, so I answered, "Such a great question deserves a well-thought-out answer. We will start there tomorrow."

My students deserve non-trivial answers, so much of my evening was spent preparing the following answer. I wanted more than transitory listening which prompted me to give students a printed copy of my answer.

The following is what I wrote and gave my students.

Got Life?

Real life is somewhat like Einstein relativity, even if inappropriately applied. *It all depends on how you look at it and who is doing the observing.* Even though Einstein's theory applies only to the speed of light, this concept leads some observers of life to reach the dangerously incorrect idea that it doesn't matter what you believe, just that you believe it with sincerity.

This is heavy stuff.

Let's get something straight here. There are some people who live lives that are far removed from the kind of person they really want to be. From a psychological perspective, these people become the kind of person they THINK other people want them to be.

If you are not dedicated to become who YOU really want yourself to be, you will gradually adopt the actions and attitudes that you believe your friends want you to be.

Developing this type of personality leads only to a life of confusion and eventually to despair.

It does not matter what constraints you are burdened with right now. You are the only one who can choose to EARN the right and purpose to live the kind of successful life you know is possible.

In life, there is a simple fact.
Your mind matters most.

In life, most self-inflicted negative circumstances happen when we don't think. Something happens, and we react without a shred of thinking. For instance, you are riding with a group of friends, and someone brings out a joint. The next thing you know, the police arrive and your parents are having chats with social services.

Similarly, you and your boyfriend or girlfriend are alone... and nine months later there is a crying baby in the arms of a girl who is wondering why the baby-daddy walked away without a hint of helping.

The critical facts of life.

There are many characteristics of being human that separate us in remarkable ways from other living things and give us a special place in the universe.

(1) we are born... we will die... and we know it.
(2) we can love... we can hate... and we choose which one.
(3) we can create... we can consume... and we enjoy both.
(4) we can serve... we can freeload... and we continue it.

Birds tweet, humans think.

Even if you tweet, text or tell your social media friends every moment of your day, there should be some degree of thinking that goes into the messages you send. Perhaps your biggest problem of the day might be finding an outlet to recharge your smartphone. In any case, there are bigger, more insightful questions that live within us.

(1) How did we get here? Are we the products of random molecular interactions or the creation of a master designer?

(2) Why are we here? Is the "pursuit of happiness" limited to self-indulgent enjoyment, or does "happiness" have a larger meaning we need to explore?

(3) Can one person make a difference? Is there any meaning to life?

In a global environment with billions of people, what does it matter?

Really?

(4) Does True Truth exist? In a society where those who disagree with others are labeled "haters," how can effective and meaningful dialogue occur?

(5) Where are we going? When we exhale for the last time, do we simply become a pile of chemicals or does some inner nature continue living?

An interesting sequel occurred involving the same boy who asked the initial question. He was one of those interesting students who irritated many teachers by his "squirrely" attitude, (No definition needed. Every teacher knows.) always trying to upstage the teacher in some way.

Near the end of the year, he blurted out at the beginning of class, "Mr. H, you gotta take those things you tell us and put 'em into one of your ebooks. You gotta title it like you end your stuff."

Thus was born my teen-oriented ebook, *Get a Grip – Join Life*.

So step one in starting a Cultural Revolution in Education is obvious.

**Our professional priority
must focus on the character development
of the individual student.**

Chap. 10 - Of this we are Certain

Abhijit Naskar

The death of George Floyd, a black man, by a white policeman was horrifying, documented and caused intense protests. Every newscast for weeks showed various people saying, "This is so wrong."

Not long into the peaceful protesting a violent rioting situation began to occur. Destruction of others' property, attacking police officers and even death of innocent people occurred. Worse yet, those who objected to such acts were called racist and the unlawful acts themselves were called the new expression of freedom of speech.

Overnight, historical "wrongs" became the new freedoms.

Whatever Happened to Truth?

Actually, **nothing** happened to truth. Truth still exists. It's just that the prevalent selfishness of individuals has grown into an overwhelming influence on society to the degree that living a relativistic lifestyle has become normal. Not only has "do my own thing" become acceptable, but intimidation by protest and being labeled HATER has stifled most counter-arguments.

Do you see the irony in the two instances noted above? Floyd's death correctly being labeled "wrong," and then calling obviously wrong destruction of other's property as now being a newly defined "freedom of expression?"

Delusions of Logic.

Our students are not stupid. When contradictory decisions are made, even applauded, they know. Students may not react, but they recognize the incongruity a relativistic worldview creates.

On a July 23, 2020 YouTube, Glenn Beck interviewed a teacher who had been fired for a Twitter post.

> *High school teacher and coach Justin Kucera is beloved by most students. He's never had charges of disciplinary action while teaching, and his students say he teaches social studies in an apolitical way. But despite his clean record, Kucera was just fired after tweeting:* **"I'm done being silent. Trump is our president."** *The Twitter mob strikes again.*

During the video, Beck commented on two other teachers in the same district who made inflammatory anti-Trump comments on FaceBook, but were not fired.

The real issue here is not a political preference; rather it is speaking up against a relativistic viewpoint producing a transitory "truth." Individually generated truth not based on any objective standard inevitably leads to conflict and illogical conclusions.

Our students see such irony. Unfortunately, the wrong message is implanted in their lifestyle, and they emulate the relativistic worldview exemplified by a significant number of our twenty-first century culture.

Relativism: An Absolute Oxymoron.

Recently, in a college class, one of my students was aggressively defending the concept that strong belief in any topic or concept produced the believer's **truth.**

Giving him the opportunity to clarify his viewpoint I asked the question, "So are you fully confident your argument about relative truth is correct?"

"ABSOLUTELY!" was his animated reply.

The spontaneous laughter by the rest of the class punctuated the illogic inherent in defending a relativistic worldview. It is a self-defeating proposition.

In education we continually construct our own sub-set of constantly changing "standards." Performance on standardized tests identifies those who "can" do college from those who "can't." Algebra I is necessary to become an educated person, but learning how to discuss the pros and cons of abortion is forbidden.

So step two in starting a Cultural Revolution in Education is equally obvious.

Absolute Truth Exists
and our role as effective educators
is to lead our students towards a lifestyle
based on the fundamentals of absolute truth.

The Ultimate Standard

When new programs are introduced you often hear two conflicting words. Administration and profit-driven publishers tout the "increased standards" inherent in the new program. Teachers often shout the inverse. "Our standards will be lowered."

Those lamenting cries illustrate how academic standards are far removed from being standard. Decade upon decade they disappear and resurface with a new identifying name.

The educational culture keeps crying for new and effective standards, yet rejects the one standard which truly is standard.

God Exists!

Let's be clear about this. Our entire culture has exerted extraordinary effort to de-standardize the thought that God is eternally alive and well.

The phrase "cancel culture" is rather recent, but the concept has been operable for quite some time.

Political correctness, cancel culture and simply not wanting to acknowledge Higher Power than our own selfish desires has resulted in a slow, but profound change in our perception of life. This change has not been violent, rather the "happiness" for little kids and adults has been maintained even while the true meaning of actual events has been hijacked.

- Merry Christmas has become Happy Holidays.
- Images of a newly born Jesus have been replaced by an overweight old man in a red suit driving flying reindeer.
- Easter has devolved into furry little rabbits laying multi-colored eggs.
- God was legally kicked out of public schools in 1962.

Perhaps the most egregious was the movement forcing the posting of the Ten Commandments from Federal Courthouses.

Even though the Declaration of Independence contains the statement, "We hold these truths to be self-evident, that all men are created equal, that they are endowed by their Creator with certain unalienable Rights…" people fight to make it politically incorrect to mention our country was founded with a reasonable focus on Judeo-Christian principles.

The Power of Evidence.

Powerful research has occurred validating historical accuracy of accounts in the Bible. From archaeological confirmations to secular writings verifying the story of Jesus, the literal account of biblical writing has been strongly supported.

While not a biblical scholar, Ronald Reagan gave personal support to the benefit of the Bible in his own life by saying, *Within the covers of the Bible are the answers for all the problems men face.*

A strong source of intuitive evidence becomes obvious as we observe the nature of the universe from the infinitesimal to the infinite. The logic of Intelligent Design transcends the necessary randomness of molecular evolution.

The intent of this book is not to explore the case for God, but if the reader wants to follow up along that line, I strongly suggest *Cold Case Christianity* by J. Warner Wallace.

Step three in starting a Cultural Revolution in Education is critical in providing the necessary ingredient to helping our students create a successfully rewarding life for themselves and others.

**God Exists
and provides the
necessary standards
giving real meaning to life.**

Chap. 11 - In Conclusion…

"If you want to build a ship,
don't drum up the men to gather wood, divide the work, and give orders.
Instead, teach them to yearn for the vast and endless sea."

<u>Antoine de Saint-Exupéry,</u>
French writer and pioneering aviator.

The purpose of this book is NOT to convince the reader to agree with all of my ideas and arguments. The purpose IS to encourage the educational community to initiate an honest and open dialogue about the following questions.

1. Are we really teaching to individuals, not groups?
2. Along with subject-matter content, are we teaching ideas and concepts providing foundation for successful lives?
3. Is what we are teaching based on Absolute Truth?
4. If the truth is suspect or ill-defined, do we address the alternative ideas or theories?

Learning From History.

Our country was founded on the principles of individual freedom existing within the structure of moral authority and minimal governmental control. Those principles are being openly violated by a relativistic lifestyle for individuals and a government subverted by extreme leftists, socialists and Marxists.

In a similar fashion, the educational system of America started as individuals in local communities who controlled the operation of their schools through local elections.

Though school board elections still occur, the nature of education has been hijacked by two opposing forces. Presently, high level governmental structure and upper administration dictate methodology, philosophy and economic control.

Equally controlling is the political and philosophical agenda of teachers' unions, often promoting a predominant liberal agenda designed to placate as many of the diverse groups in the local population. Trying to be effective for various stakeholders is a good thing, but never at the expense of abandoning the solid foundations on which education started.

A Necessary Revolution.

> *"Here's to the crazy ones, the misfits, the rebels, the troublemakers, the round pegs in the square holes ... the ones who see things differently -- they're not fond of rules, and they have no respect for the status quo. ... You can quote them, disagree with them, glorify or vilify them, but the only thing you can't do is ignore them because they change things. ... They push the human race forward, and while some may see them as the crazy ones, we see genius, because the people who are crazy enough to think that they can change the world, are the ones who do."*

Steve Jobs

The American Revolution became possible only as individuals became involved. Farmers, business owners, laborers needed to become committed enough to take up arms, leave their families and confront the British. This happened and the world was changed.

Similarly, a cultural revolution in American education must be initiated and accomplished as individual teachers and administrators catch the vision of true reform. Individuals must choose courage and begin to reestablish those principles of human interaction which produce positive results in their students.

The challenge is huge. Not only are governmental systems and teachers' unions entrenched in the system, but any improvement in the inertial stagnation of the system is stifled by the natural consequences of the mediocrity and apathy taught by the present system.

Do you get it?

Constant application of an educational system which produces students seeped in apathy and mediocrity guarantees the continuance of the system. Add to that the cultural intimidation of political correctness and stifling of counter-thought and the *status quo* is guaranteed.

The increasing advent of online learning further decreases the ability to create positive change, especially in the arena of HOPE learning. As "content-only" learning becomes the norm, the living principles of life become much harder to incorporate into the total program.

Competing Revolutions.

Welcome to the Revolution Party. There are already culture changing revolutions happening and we are watching and experiencing them live.

The most obvious revolution currently displayed on all our devices is the attempt to radically transform our form of government. Peaceful protests under the pretense of Black Lives Matter have been infiltrated by subversive groups (Antifa, for one?) working to change our republic into a more socialistic state. The worth of independent initiative is being demeaned and governmental control of wealth, health and activity is being promoted.

A seemingly positive revolution is well-along in its implementation. The mind-boggling advance of Artificial Intelligence is making life easier and more productive, appearing to be a welcome advance in our daily living. Actually I used the wrong modifier in calling this revolution "mind-boggling." If we are not alert to unintended consequences, this AI revolution will become mind-numbing! We will become accustomed to machines doing our thinking and will be victims of the "Intellectual Caste System" in which a very small group of creative individuals will produce devices and systems consumed by the majority of us, thus decreasing our ability to use our own creativity and initiative.

An alarming sub-set of the Artificial Intelligence revolution is happening not just before our eyes but within our profession. The teachers who "stand before their students" is being replaced by flat-screens and mouse-directed decisions. We need to shift our response to online learning from "that's really cool" to "where will this be in five years?" Without assertive action, we may become the last generation of classroom teachers.

Action Versus Acquiescence

"It is unthinkable in the twentieth century to fail to distinguish between what constitutes an abominable atrocity that must be prosecuted and what constitutes that "past" which "ought not to be stirred up."

We have to condemn publicly the very idea that some people have the right to repress others. In keeping silent about evil, in burying it so deep within us that no sign of it appears on the surface, we are implanting it, and it will rise up a thousandfold in the future. When we neither punish nor reproach evildoers, we are not simply protecting their trivial old age, we are thereby ripping the foundations of justice from beneath new generations. It is for this reason, and not because of the "weakness of indoctrinational work," that they are growing up "indifferent." Young people are acquiring the conviction that foul deeds are never punished on earth, that they always bring prosperity.
It is going to be uncomfortable, horrible, to live in such a country!"

— *Aleksandr Solzhenitsyn, The Gulag Archipelago 1918–1956*

Solzhenitsyn's ordeal far exceeded that which we currently face. We are not facing starvation, death or designated toilet time, but the results of allowing the present culture of our time to flourish may be equally devastating.

A continuing theme of The Gulag Archipelago was the quiet acquiescence of normal citizens as the Marxist atrocities continued.

We must not stand quietly on the sidelines while immersed in the quiet culture as the essence of our professional experience is being negated, thus eliminating true benefit from our students. We need to stand up, speak out and take action to prevent the flame of our passions being extinguished by hierarchy and technology.

There is a Way.

Perhaps our initial actions seem inconsequential, but they might be equivalent to a Boston Tea Party event. We must start the Cultural Revolution in Education.

There are several practical steps we can take, each one as simple, yet profound, as tossing a bale of tea into the bay.

1. Vote for governmental officials who understand the need for genuine reform in education.

2. Do not fear school choice. Competition will result in comprehensive improvement.

3. Encourage the implementation of Lateral Leadership, creating a shared decision making system within our own schools.

4. As professional teachers, trust your logic and your heart to speak up and stand out when you see injustice and inefficiency in the system.

5. Choose the courage to teach not just subject-matter content, but include the HOPE needed to produce genuinely successful students.

6. If we are serious about wanting higher standards in education, do not fear God being reinstated into the education system.

Be Brave. Become Revolutionary.
Become Radically Excellent.

Final Thoughts from the Author

There are ominous cultural restrictions on the freedom to engage in productive debate and discussion. Political correctness, the "cancel culture," unwarranted "truth" as established by some scientists and a misguided "tolerance" expectation make it dangerous, or at least intimidating, to speak freely about important issues.

Combine those issues with the chaos of opening schools during a Covid-19 pandemic, and the very nature of education appears to be at a watershed moment.

Change is inevitable, and we need to use the change as an opportunity to be part of a change enhanccing the lifetime benefit of education for our students.

We are important and expert in the profession of teaching. We must not stand by and do nothing as external people and events allow our profession to be hijacked by politicians, publishers and even teachers' unions.

Frankly, it isn't only our students at intellectual risk. Teacher jobs are equally threatened, especially as online learning becomes the norm. It is a guarantee Artificial Intelligence is going to become the provider of content-learning with a minimal human interaction, mostly by clerical type humans. Who knows? Perhaps in five years unused school buildings will have parking lots filled with WalMart and Target shopping carts as formerly homeless and their dogs will occupy the rooms.

Change is coming. We cannot deny that fact. What we must do, however, is cause our voices to assist and direct that change. In using our voice we must transcend the level of "only one student to the bathroom at a time" discussions. We needed to address larger relevent issues.

We need to envelop TRUTH by dissusing all sides of issues.

Character traits of successful accomplishers must be stressed.

We need to encourage, even teach, proper rhetoric among students.

Can Old be Revolutionary?

The ancient Greek system of learning focused on the use of the Trivium, essentially meaning the three (Tri...) roads (via...) to learning. Bryan Maertzdorf summarized the nature of the Trivium in a Facebook post on May 18, 2017.

The Trivium

1. **Grammar** (grammar stage) or ***Knowledge*** – Learning the body of knowledge of a subject. (Answers the question of Who, What, Where, and When).

Grammar is the first building block to integrated, objective knowledge. The body of knowledge, when gathered and arranged under the rules of general grammar can then be subjected to logic for full understanding, which is a separate intellectual procedure.

2. **Logic** (dialectic stage) or ***Understanding*** – Learning to reason. (Answers the question of Why).

Logic or reasoning is practiced by establishing valid (non-contradictory) relationships among facts, leading to systematic understanding. This tool is used for thinking correctly; without contradiction (includes the identification of logical fallacies. *See previous Blogs on fallacies Part 1 and 2*). The goal of logic is proof and consists of establishing the truth and validity of a concept or proposition in agreement with objective, factual reality.

Note: The body of knowledge learned in the grammar stage is used to practice reasoning in the Logic (dialectic) stage. In the Logic stage we try to understand the facts we learned in the grammar stage.

3. **Rhetoric** (rhetoric stage) or ***Wisdom*** – Learning the science of non-violent communication and the art of expression. (Provides the How of a subject).

Rhetoric or Wisdom is the application and expression of knowledge and understanding (conclusions reached from the prior stages of grammar and logic) on a subject.

Summary: In the grammar stage the facts are learned; in the logic (dialectic) stage we began to understand those facts, and in the rhetoric stage we learn to express what we now understand.

There are two ways to look at the Trivium: 1-the learning stages that correspond to a child's cognitive development, and, 2-the natural process that is followed when a person of any age learns something new.

The first way is the definable progression of a child's development. In the first stage (grammar [memorization of facts], corresponds to the elementary grades) there is a natural affinity for storing up substantial amounts of information on a variety of subjects, from nursery rhymes to math facts, and recalling that information at will. The next stage (logic or dialectic [understanding and analytical thinking], corresponds to the junior high grades), the ability to reason is refined, and facts learned in the grammar stage are used as an exercise in argumentation. The last stage (rhetoric [expression and abstract thinking], corresponds to the high school grades), self-discovery and expression are the focus, and cognitive abilities reach their full maturity.

He followed that with an excellent discourse on the mystical relationship the ancient Greeks had with the 3-4-5 triangle and its involvement in the aspect of learning.

One interpretation of the mystical quality of this special triangle is as follows:
    3 = Trivium – Classical Education (First 3 of the 7 Liberal Arts), 1-Grammar, 2-Logic and 3-Rhetoric.
4 = Quadrivium – Classical Education (Next 4 of the 7 Liberal Arts): 4-Arithmetic, 5-Geometry, 6-Music and 7-Astronomy.
5 = Senses – the methods of experience to learn. Taste, sight, smell, hear and touch.
As stated in Part I, **the goal of classical education was to teach "how" to think, not "what" to think, resulting in an autodidactic (self-taught) society**. A society of "thinkers." These integrated tools of learning could be applied to any subject encountered. In contrast, modern education teaches memorization, aka "what" to think, resulting in society of compliant "workers."

Perhaps building a model of education based on those ancient Greek ideals would actually work as we emerge from the pandemic universe. Logically (no pun intended) this will never be implemented in one revolutionary moment. A better idea is to start, as individuals, by incorporating those principles into our daily lessons.

One teacher at a time, one day at a time... once the transition becomes exponential, revolutionary change might actually occur. The worst-case scenario could be the equivalent of one starfish. And that would be a good thng.

Doing the same fixes year after year hasn't worked.

Maybe, just maybe...